International Series in Operations Research & Management Science

Volume 294

Series Editor

Camille C. Price
Department of Computer Science, Stephen F. Austin State University, Nacogdoches, TX, USA

Associate Editor

Joe Zhu
Foisie Business School, Worcester Polytechnic Institute, Worcester, MA, USA

Founding Editor

Frederick S. Hillier
Stanford University, Stanford, CA, USA

More information about this series at http://www.springer.com/series/6161

Pekka J. Korhonen • Jyrki Wallenius

Making Better Decisions

Balancing Conflicting Criteria

 Springer

Pekka J. Korhonen
Aalto University School of Business
Espoo, Finland

Jyrki Wallenius
Aalto University School of Business
Espoo, Finland

ISSN 0884-8289   ISSN 2214-7934 (electronic)
International Series in Operations Research & Management Science
ISBN 978-3-030-49457-5   ISBN 978-3-030-49459-9 (eBook)
https://doi.org/10.1007/978-3-030-49459-9

© Springer Nature Switzerland AG 2020
This work is subject to copyright. All rights are reserved by the Publisher, whether the whole or part of the material is concerned, specifically the rights of translation, reprinting, reuse of illustrations, recitation, broadcasting, reproduction on microfilms or in any other physical way, and transmission or information storage and retrieval, electronic adaptation, computer software, or by similar or dissimilar methodology now known or hereafter developed.
The use of general descriptive names, registered names, trademarks, service marks, etc. in this publication does not imply, even in the absence of a specific statement, that such names are exempt from the relevant protective laws and regulations and therefore free for general use.
The publisher, the authors, and the editors are safe to assume that the advice and information in this book are believed to be true and accurate at the date of publication. Neither the publisher nor the authors or the editors give a warranty, expressed or implied, with respect to the material contained herein or for any errors or omissions that may have been made. The publisher remains neutral with regard to jurisdictional claims in published maps and institutional affiliations.

This Springer imprint is published by the registered company Springer Nature Switzerland AG.
The registered company address is: Gewerbestrasse 11, 6330 Cham, Switzerland

*To our personal decision-makers
Kaiju and Hannele,
who have enriched our lives in uncountable
ways*

Preface

Decision-making is one of the key functions of managers in private and public organizations. Moreover, human beings in their private or personal lives face numerous small and large decisions. Good decisions are important for organizations and human beings; bad decisions may be devastating. Sometimes you may not know (until much later) whether you have made a good or a bad decision. However, a human being is not a machine. As the ancient Romans used to say: "Errare humanum est, sed in errare perseverare diabolicum," which translates to: "To err is human, but to persist in error is diabolical." Humans do not always learn from their mistakes. A decision problem may be very complex, making it impossible to understand all its features. This is understandable. However—and this is unfortunate—people often make bad choices even in relatively simple situations.

In everyday decision situations, most of our decisions are based on intuition. For instance, in a supermarket we do not proceed to analyze which criteria to use in buying apples or oranges. Nor do we normally spend much time analyzing where to go for dinner. Intuition is a wonderful thing. Much of creative work is based on the use of intuition. Unfortunately, as we will document in this book, intuition has its faults and limitations, and its sole use may not always lead to good outcomes. We will show that some form of analysis (even simple), often combined with intuitive thinking, will prove invaluable.

This book is about decision-making. There are several books which deal with decision-making, some by very famous authors. The main focus of these books is, in general, on decision-making under uncertainty and the difficulties humans experience processing probabilities. As for the methodology, most of the existing books use decision analysis, a formal approach based on eliciting decision-maker's probabilities and utilities.

Our focus is on decision-making in the presence of multiple criteria. Generally, decisions are based on multiple decision criteria, which are explicitly considered or implicitly present in the decision-making process. Even in corporate contexts, where an organization is interested in maximizing its profits, it has to consider other criteria, such as risk and employee satisfaction. The prevalence of multiple criteria is obvious in public sector decision-making. Multiple criteria generally play a secondary or minor role in existing books dealing with decision-making.

When we talk about aiding decision-makers, it is not only about mathematics, although mathematics does play an important role. The bounded rationality of humans, using the term coined by Herbert Simon, also plays a large role in decision-making. Behavioral aspects are at the core of decision-making. Accordingly, we discuss behavioral aspects of decision-making at length in our book.

Decision-making in the presence of multiple criteria appears rather straightforward. Practitioners often just give importance weights to the criteria, multiply each criterion value with its weight, and add up. However, as our discussion shows, our field is far from being simple. It is a field which has hidden traps and complications. It is our purpose to forewarn the reader about them! Forewarned is forearmed!

In our book, we discuss the following issues, mostly in the context of multiple criteria decision-making:

1. The use of intuition vs. more analytic approach
2. How do humans make decisions when facing conflicting criteria
3. Why humans err and how to avoid well-known pitfalls
4. Psychological aspects of managerial decision-making
5. How to make better decisions and how to make wise decisions (the essence of multiple criteria decision-making)
6. How to put visual representations into good use
7. How to negotiate wisely

Our book is intended for practicing managers in the same spirit as Kahneman's best-selling book *Thinking, Fast and Slow*, 2011 We use material based on our research extending over 40 years, including some recent research. We also use some material from the master's seminars and lectures delivered by Korhonen on multiple criteria decision-making at the Helsinki School of Economics during 1979–1986. Some material is also utilized from lectures delivered by Wallenius on behavioral decision-making during 2006–2014 and negotiation analysis during 2017–2019 at Aalto University School of Business. We seek to review all background information in not too technical way, which is necessary for understanding the contents of the book. Even though the book is primarily intended for practicing managers, we hope that it is interesting reading also for PhD students, faculty in business and engineering schools, and the general public at large, interested in decision-making. In addition to conceptual discussions, our book includes numerous illustrative examples. The book can also be used as a textbook. Only a modest mathematical background is needed to understand its main principles.

Readers who are not so familiar with mathematics can easily read the main part of each chapter, in which we conceptually or visually approach the subject. The reader may skip the appendices, which use some mathematics to illustrate our ideas more precisely and seek to deepen our understanding of the underlying phenomena.

Why This Book?

Why did we want to write this book? What differentiates it from other books on decision-making? We feel that we have something important to say, which is not covered in other books, namely the complexities in balancing conflicting criteria. We adopt a broad perspective on decision-making and do not limit ourselves to using some specific methodology or technique, such as decision trees or linear programming. We think that practicing managers can benefit from reading our book. They daily face situations, where they have to balance conflicting criteria. Managers need help. It is also interesting and useful for all of us to attempt to improve our daily decision-making.

Where Does Our Interest Come From?

Jyrki Wallenius wrote his PhD thesis about multiple criteria decision-making in 1975 and published two chapters as journal articles in *Management* Science, one single authored and the other jointly with Stanley Zionts. They came out in 1975 and 1976. Pekka Korhonen and Jyrki Wallenius began to collaborate in the late 1970s— on negotiations and multiple criteria decision-making. Our goal has always been to develop realistic decision support systems that managers would find useful. To accomplish this, we realized rather early on that we should better understand how people actually make choices and make the computer systems more compatible with the way humans behave. One of our first behavioral papers was published with Professor Herbert Moskowitz, Purdue University, in the *Annals of Operations Research* in 1990.

In the late 1980s and early 1990s, we jointly ran a master's thesis seminar at the former Helsinki School of Economics, focusing on behavioral aspects in multiple criteria decision-making. Our seminar produced over 10 master's theses. We published journal articles on some, but not nearly all of them. In our book, we discuss both our published and unpublished work.

Why Us?

What makes the two of us qualified for writing this book and providing advice to practicing managers, PhD students, faculty, and other readers? Collectively, we have over 85 years of experience in conducting research in multiple criteria decision-making. Our experience and first publications date back to the 1970s. We have developed algorithms, carried out theoretical work, built computer-based decision support systems, and applied our knowledge to interesting practical problems in private and public organizations. We have extensively published in world-class journals. We have consulted organizations. We have served in leadership roles in the International Society on Multiple Criteria Decision Making.

Organization of the Book

The focus of our book is mainly (although not exclusively) on riskless choice. This book is organized as follows.

Chapter 1 discusses different paradigms of decision-making. Chapter 2 highlights the role and limitations of intuition. Chapter 3 introduces analytic decision-making and in particular multiple criteria decision-making. Chapter 4 deals with descriptive decision theory: in other words, how humans make decisions. Chapters 5 and 6 focus on biases and decision traps in decision-making under certainty and uncertainty, respectively. Chapter 7 discusses additional details about analytic decision-making and in particular multiple criteria decision-making. Chapter 8 overviews some basic visualization techniques that are helpful in multiple criteria decision-making. Chapter 9 focuses on decision problems, where we know all decision alternatives. Chapters 10 and 11 discuss so-called design problems, where the decision alternatives have been described with the help of a mathematical model. Chapter 12 overviews several computer-based decision support systems, which we have developed. Chapter 13 discusses the use of scenarios to model uncertainty in decision-making. Chapter 14 introduces the reader to efficiency analysis. Chapter 15 deals with several real-world applications, in which we have been involved. Chapter 16 discusses the related problem of negotiations or group decision-making, both in win-lose and win-win situations. Chapter 17 concludes our book.

Espoo, Finland   Pekka J. Korhonen
Espoo, Finland   Jyrki Wallenius
March 2020

Acknowledgments

We wish to thank Mr. Tapio Aaltonen, for reading and commenting parts of the book. His advice has proven invaluable. We also thank Emeritus Professor Stanley Zionts for letting us rather freely borrow from some of our joint unpublished papers. Jyrki Wallenius also wishes to acknowledge the long collaboration with Stanley Zionts, who originally was Jyrki's PhD supervisor at the European Institute for Advanced Studies in Management, Brussels. Many of our joint ideas are described in this book. We would also like to thank Professor Juuso Liesiö and Jyrki's daughter, Professor Johanna Wallenius, for useful comments regarding the writing of our book.

We wish to collectively thank all our collaborators and former students, who have been a constant source of inspiration to us over the years. We also wish to thank the Foundation of the Helsinki School of Economics for financially supporting us over the years.

We extend our heartfelt thanks to Christian Rauscher from Springer Verlag for giving us the opportunity to write this book and for all his support during the process.

Contents

1	**Different Paradigms of Decision-Making**		1
	1.1	Vision-Based Decision-Making	2
	1.2	Rule-Based Decision-Making	3
	References		4
2	**About the Role of Intuition**		5
	2.1	Background	5
	2.2	Examples Where Intuition Fails	6
	2.3	How About Using Both Intuition and Analytic Thinking	10
	Appendix: Misleading Intuition		10
	References		10
3	**Towards Analytic Decision-Making**		11
	3.1	Background	12
	3.2	Fundamental Concepts	13
	3.3	Wise Decisions	16
	3.4	Dangers of Oversimplification	18
	3.5	Wrapping up	19
	References		20
4	**How Do Humans Make Choices?**		21
	4.1	Satisficers	21
	4.2	Lexicographic Model	22
	4.3	Compensatory Models	23
	4.4	Elimination by Aspects	24
	4.5	Prospect Theory or the Reference-Dependent Model	25
	4.6	Evidence for Prospect Theory or the Riskless Version	27
	Appendix: More Details on Prospect Theory		28
		Where We Have Used Prospect Theory	29
	References		30

5	**Beware of Decision Traps: The World of Certainty**		31
	5.1	Hearing What You Want to Hear	31
	5.2	Too Much Simplification	32
	5.3	Context Matters	33
	5.4	Anchoring	35
	5.5	Not Admitting Past Mistakes	36
	5.6	Lives Saved or Lives Lost	36
	5.7	Hubris	37
	References		38
6	**Beware of Decision Traps: The World of Uncertainty**		39
	6.1	We Think We Know More Than We Actually Do	39
	6.2	Memory Plays Tricks	40
	6.3	Rare Is Rare	41
	6.4	O. J. Simpson Trial	42
	Appendix: Probability Calculations		43
	References		44
7	**The Devil Is in the Details**		45
	7.1	Alternatives	45
		7.1.1 Known Alternatives and Decision Variables	45
		7.1.2 Alternatives Emerging Over Time	46
		7.1.3 Not Realizing Viable Alternatives	47
		7.1.4 Too Many Alternatives	47
	7.2	Criteria	48
		7.2.1 One vs. Multiple Criteria	48
		7.2.2 Criteria vs. Goals and Objectives	49
		7.2.3 Attributes and Indicators	50
		7.2.4 Qualitative vs. Quantitative Criteria	50
		7.2.5 Structure of Criteria and Their Possible Dependence	51
		7.2.6 Known vs. Unknown Criteria	51
		7.2.7 Certainty vs. Uncertainty in the Criterion Values	53
	7.3	Dominance	55
	7.4	Value (or Utility)	56
	7.5	Number of Decision-Makers	57
	7.6	Design Problems	57
	7.7	Why Are Some Choices Difficult?	59
	7.8	What are Better Decisions in an MCDM Context?	60
	Appendix: Car Accident and Production Planning		60
	References		61
8	**A Picture Is Worth a Thousand Words**		63
	8.1	Visual Representation of Numerical Data	64
		8.1.1 Bar Charts, Line Graphs, and Scatter Plots	64

		8.1.2 Visualization of Multivariate Data: More Advanced Techniques	66
	8.2	Lying with Graphs	69
	8.3	Visualization in Multiple Criteria Decision Support Systems	71
		8.3.1 Snapshots of a Single Alternative	71
		8.3.2 Illustrating a Set of Alternatives/Solutions	72
	8.4	Why Visualization?	73
	Appendix: Andrews Curves		73
	References		73
9	**Choosing Among Known Alternatives**		75
	9.1	Benjamin Franklin's Approach	76
	9.2	Even Swaps	76
	9.3	Weighted Sums	78
		9.3.1 Weights and Scales	78
	9.4	Beware of Joint Effects of Similar Criteria	82
	9.5	Do Not Accidentally Eliminate the Best Alternative!	83
	9.6	The Analytic Hierarchy Process	84
		9.6.1 Formulating a Marketing Strategy for a Small IT Company	86
	9.7	Visual Interactive Method for Discrete Alternatives (VIMDA)	87
	References		88
10	**Designing Potential Solutions**		91
	10.1	Feasible Set and Nondominated Set for the Design Problem	91
	10.2	Goal Programming	94
	10.3	Appendix: Illustrating the Decision and Criterion Spaces	97
	References		99
11	**Solving Design Problems**		101
	11.1	Weighted Sums	101
	11.2	Reference Point Method	104
	11.3	Reference Direction Approach	105
	11.4	Pareto Race	107
	11.5	A Challenging Nonconvex Feasible Region	108
	11.6	Estimating Weights from Pairwise Comparisons	109
	References		110
12	**Need for Decision Support Systems**		111
	12.1	Harmonious Houses	111
	12.2	VIMDA	112
	12.3	VIG (Pareto Race)	114

12.4	Production Planning with VIG (Pareto Race)	115
12.5	A Digression: How Much Support Is Desirable?	118
References		119

13 Use Scenarios Instead of a Crystal Ball ... 121
13.1	What Is Scenario Analysis?	122
13.2	Using Scenario Analysis for Financial Institutions	123
	13.2.1 Capital and Analysis Review by the Federal Reserve	123
	13.2.2 Other Applications	125
13.3	Multiple Criteria Decision Making with Scenarios	125
13.4	Appendix: A MOLP Formulation for Investment Planning	128
References		129

14 Making Operations More Efficient ... 131
14.1	Data Envelopment Analysis	132
14.2	How to Measure Efficiency?	133
14.3	Value Efficiency	136
	14.3.1 Additional Details of Value Efficiency Analysis	137
References		139

15 Real-World Problems ... 141
15.1	Pricing Alcoholic Beverages	142
15.2	Emergency Management	142
15.3	Cost Efficiency of Finnish Electricity Distributors	143
15.4	Value Efficiency Analysis	144
	15.4.1 Case 1: Hypermarkets	144
	15.4.2 Case 2: Academic Research	145
	15.4.3 Case 3: Parishes	146
	15.4.4 Case 4: Bank Branch Efficiency	147
References		148

16 Negotiating a Deal ... 149
16.1	Win-Lose Negotiations	150
16.2	Win-Win Negotiations	151
16.3	Pre-Negotiations Are Useful	153
16.4	Real-World Examples	154
	16.4.1 To What Extent Should Energy Be Taxed?	155
	16.4.2 Should Banks and Insurance Companies Merge?	156
References		157

17 In Conclusion ... 159
17.1	Realize That Intuition May Fail You	159
17.2	If Possible, Complement Your Intuition with Some Analysis	159
17.3	Be Aware of Common Decision Traps	160
17.4	Humans Focus on Differences	160

17.5	Think Hard About All Possible Decision Alternatives		160
17.6	Think Whether You Are 'Optimizer' or 'Satisficer'		160
17.7	Be Transparent About the Criteria		160
17.8	Identify Dominated Decision Alternatives and Eliminate Them		161
17.9	Think How You Want to Express Your Preferences		161
17.10	Think About Ways to Visualize Decision Alternatives		161
17.11	Improving Efficiency of Operations		161
17.12	Use Scenarios When Facing Uncertainty		162
17.13	Figure Out What You Want and What the Other Party Wants		162

Author Index 163

Subject Index 165

Chapter 1
Different Paradigms of Decision-Making

All students of Decision Analysis and Operations Research have been taught that decision-making is choice-based, in other words it involves making choices. We have been taught that decision-makers compile a list of decision alternatives, which they evaluate with one or several criteria, often subject to uncertain states of nature (Bell et al. 1977; Olson 1996). Then they choose the best or most preferred alternative from this list, using some appropriate decision rule. In case of uncertainty, the most common decision rule corresponds to maximizing expected utility. Raiffa's book *Decision Analysis* is a wonderful example (Raiffa 1968). In case of riskless choice under multiple criteria, the decision rule may simply be a weighted average, where the weights represent the 'importance' of the criteria. Students of Decision Analysis are taught that the decision-maker knows all decision alternatives and can quantitatively evaluate them in terms of relevant criteria. Alternatively, one can implicitly define the decision alternatives via a mathematical model. In this case we talk about Multiple Criteria Decision Making or optimization. In either case, the choice from the available decision alternatives is open.

In our book we follow this old, choice-based paradigm, but in numerous places extend it by discussing behavioral realities. Our primary focus is decision problems[1] in the context of riskless choice in the presence of multiple criteria. However, it is important to realize that in the real-world, managers may follow other paradigms. We briefly discuss them.

---

[1]It is important to make a distinction between a decision problem and a 'worry' problem. Being worried, whether it is going to rain in the afternoon, is a typical worry problem. There is nothing you can do about the weather. Hence there is no decision involved. We face a decision problem, if we consider whether or not to take an umbrella with us to town.

1.1 Vision-Based Decision-Making

Not all decision problems involve an open comparison of alternatives, as suggested by the choice-based paradigm. It is not uncommon that the leader has chosen a course of action based on her vision, or perhaps the leader was hired based on her vision. There is no evaluation of alternatives. Other alternatives may not even be seriously considered. The leader either fails or succeeds with her vision. Typically, the leader falls for the so-called confirming evidence bias, in other words looks for and listens to advice, which supports her prior views on the superiority of the chosen course of action. Moreover, it is not uncommon in such cases that the leader hires people who she knows will support her views, and whose job it is to muster the required support for the vision. We call such a decision-making paradigm vision-based.

Now, acting based upon a vision, may be dangerous. It is important to understand, on what the vision is based. If the vision is solely based on the leader's intuition, the risks are high. We think that all people in leadership positions should use the devil's advocate[2] approach. In other words, listen to people who can challenge and test the original vision. The devil's advocate should question original forecasts about costs and revenues, and also what we think our competitors will do. The devil's advocate should generate additional alternatives and ask why not. If, after being exposed to the devil's advocate's ideas and arguments, the boss still feels that her original idea is good, at minimum she has a better confidence in her decision. And if things turn sour, she is in a better position to defend her decision. The approach adopted by the devil's advocate may also be called a feasibility test. The concept of a feasibility test is well-known among engineers. Bridges undergo feasibility tests! Then why not important corporate decisions?

All leaders would benefit from dissenting views (the devil's advocate), which can test the vision, and help in many problems of implementation. A bit of modeling may also help confirm the choice. For example, we may explicitly identify criteria, which make the chosen alternative most preferred. The key question is, do such criteria stand open scrutiny. Our point is that the vision-based decision paradigm is highly risky, unless the vision is based on careful prior analysis.

We illustrate with a real-world decision problem of this type. Unfortunately, we do not know on what the leader's vision in this case was based on.

---

[2]According to the Wikipedia, the Devil's advocate (in Latin Advocatus Diaboli) was formerly an official position within the Catholic Church: one who "argued against the sainthood of a candidate in order to uncover any character flaws or misrepresentation of the evidence favoring canonization".

Example 1.1 Changing the Logo and Trademark of Service Station Chains
The company was originally in the business of refining oil in Finland, where it enjoyed a monopolistic position. The business had gradually been expanded to include retail marketing of oil products. Over time, the company purchased 50% of two gas station chains, consisting of service stations and unmanned stations. Since 1982, the increase in the market share was the company's main long-term criterion. As a result, by 1989, the company owned between 50% and 98% of three nationwide gas station chains.

The vision of the responsible division head was that the company should have all service and automated stations that it owned under the company's own name and logo. He had had this vision ten years earlier. He thought that having three different smaller chains was inefficient. Rationalization was needed to improve profitability. Once ownership in these chains had been acquired, during the latter part of the 1980s, the question became as to what extent, how and when to implement the strategy of a unified logo, and what it would cost. The company was concerned about (not) reinforcing its "monopoly image" through the operation. After extensive preparations, a go-ahead decision was taken in the summer of 1991. Two station chains would change their logo, but the third would continue operations as before under its own logo. The third chain enjoyed a good (distinct) reputation, and the company decided not to risk reinforcing the monopolistic image, which the change of the logo for all stations would have implied. The decision concerned approximately 800 service and unmanned stations. At the same time, the stations were modernized.

The decision process neither represented a series of "classical" rational decisions, nor "muddling through". The management had a clear early vision of what it wanted the company to become. Once opportunities arose, they were seized. The criteria were also clear. Long-term profitability was of primary concern, as was becoming more "customer driven". The decision to prepare and plan the change in logo was made as early as 1989 to allow for careful planning. The final decision to implement the plan was made as late as possible without endangering the implementation operation (summer 1991). An important part of the decision process was mustering support for the idea among company's own employees, dealers and station personnel (Excerpted from Kasanen et al. 2000).

1.2 Rule-Based Decision-Making

In the corporate world, we also often talk about rule-based decision-making, although not typically at higher levels. The management has come up with a set of rules for 'lower-level' employees to follow. There are also many rule-based decision tools, called expert systems. Their idea is to allow people to learn and make decisions like experts. Their advantages also include that they are very structured, and do not require special skills to use. Moreover, the rules are documented, allowing for accountability. Rules also have their cons. As the expertise of the individual grows, she may 'outgrow' the rules. For employees, it may be boring and inflexible simply to follow rules. For additional details about rule-based decision-making we ask the reader to consult the book by James March: *Primer on Decision Making* (March 1994). March was a prominent organization theorist.

We illustrate rule-based decision-making with two examples. A simple case in point is the rule to ask for an ID of a person at a cash register, if what she is paying exceeds 50 euros. In that case the person sitting at the cash register does not have to make any decisions, just to follow the rule. If the person paying gets upset, when asked to provide with an ID, the salesperson can fall back on the rule (company policy). A more complex example refers to quality control and the operation of a production line. Assume that the production line conducts quality controls of every 100th item produced by the line. If in a day, you encounter two or more defective products, take the issue up with the management. This rule is most likely based on statistical quality control.

Note that the management must have decided about the rules. It may not be trivial to decide about rules. This is a specific and complex decision problem. We think it is a good question to pose, what are "optimal rules"? What criteria to use in designing rules? How many rules and for what situations should we have rules? The management also needs to decide, when old rules should be revised. These are all interesting questions; however, we do not discuss them in our book.

References

Bell, D., Keeney, R. L., & Raiffa, H. (1977). *Conflicting objectives in decisions*. Chichester: Wiley.
Kasanen, E., Wallenius, H., Wallenius, J., & Zionts, S. (2000). A study of high-level managerial decision processes. *European Journal of Operational Research, 120*(3), 496–510.
March, J. (1994). *Primer on decision making: How decisions happen*. New York: Free Press.
Olson, D. (1996). *Decision aids for selection problems*. New York: Springer.
Raiffa, H. (1968). *Decision analysis*. Reading, MA: Addison-Wesley.

Chapter 2
About the Role of Intuition

2.1 Background

Intuition is a very necessary element of creative work, such as research. Many famous scientists have discussed the role of intuition in their work. We provide two quotes.

> "Isaac Newton supposedly watched an apple fall from a tree and suddenly connected its motion as being caused by the same universal gravitational force that governs the moon's attraction to the earth." John Maynard Keynes, the famous economist, said "Newton owed his success to his muscles of intuition. Newton's powers ..." (www.p-i-a.com/Magazine/Issue19/Physics_19.htm).

Gigerenzer, author of the book *Gut Feelings: The Intelligence of the Unconscious* (2008), claims that he is both intuitive and rational. "In my scientific work, I have hunches. I can't explain always why I think a certain path is the right way, but I need to trust it and go ahead. I also have the ability to check these hunches and find out what they are about. That's the science part. Now, in private life, I rely on instinct. For instance, when I first met my wife, I didn't do computations. Nor did she." (B. Kasanoff in *Forbes Magazine* February 21st, 2017.)

But the difference between research and decision-making is that, intuition often guides research, but is subsequently subjected to rigorous laboratory and field tests. We ask that the same is done about the use of intuition in decision-making. Because solely basing your decisions (in particular, in the corporate context) on intuition, is very risky—and unnecessary. If possible, one should do some form of analysis, either to help support the intuition or challenge it. This chapter serves as motivation for us, why we often benefit from some form of analysis.

Daniel Kahneman was interviewed on May 25th, 2012, for the *Spiegel Online Magazine* about the role of intuition in decision-making. The interview is interesting and we reproduce here the beginning of it (Also see Kahneman 2011).

SPIEGEL: By studying human intuition, or System 1, you seem to have learned to distrust this intuition ...

Kahneman: I wouldn't put it that way. Our intuition works very well for the most part. But it's interesting to examine where it fails.

SPIEGEL: Experts, for example, have gathered a lot of experience in their respective fields and, for this reason, are convinced that they have very good intuition about their particular field. Shouldn't we be able to rely on that?

Kahneman: It depends on the field. In the stock market, for example, the predictions of experts are practically worthless. Anyone who wants to invest money is better off choosing index funds, which simply follow a certain stock index without any intervention of gifted stock pickers. Year after year, they perform better than 80% of the investment funds managed by highly paid specialists. Nevertheless, intuitively, we want to invest our money with somebody who appears to understand, even though the statistical evidence is plain that they are very unlikely to do so. Of course, there are fields in which expertise exists. This depends on two things: whether the domain is inherently predictable, and whether the expert has had sufficient experience to learn the regularities. The world of stock is inherently unpredictable.

...

SPIEGEL: Do we generally put too much faith in experts?

Kahneman: I'm not claiming that the predictions of experts are fundamentally worthless. ... Take doctors. They're often excellent when it comes to short-term predictions. But they're often quite poor in predicting how a patient will be doing in 5 or 10 years. And they don't know the difference. That's the key.

Can investment advisers and doctors be trusted? We are sure that the answer depends on who you ask. Regarding investment advisers, we tend to agree with Kahneman. Regarding experienced doctors, we think we have to trust them. But they need diagnostic tests, possibly the help of Artificial Intelligence (in the future). The medical doctors are notoriously poor in understanding probabilities. We discuss an example below.

The answer to the question, whose intuitive judgments can be trusted, obviously depends on the field. If the field (or phenomenon) is mature and its structure and causal laws are understandable and clear, and the person is an experienced professional, we can have more trust in her intuition.

2.2 Examples Where Intuition Fails

In many cases our intuition fails. We provide some examples.

2.2 Examples Where Intuition Fails

Example 2.1 Mouse and Rope
Assume that a red rope is spanned around a soccer ball (case A in Fig. 2.1). Because the circumference of the ball is about 70 cm, it is also the length of the rope. Let's take a new rope of length 170 cm (which is exactly 1 m longer than the previous rope) and make a circle out of it. Span this circle evenly around the ball in such a way that the distance from the circle to the surface of the ball is always the same (case B). Is it possible that a mouse can run on the surface of the ball without touching the rope?

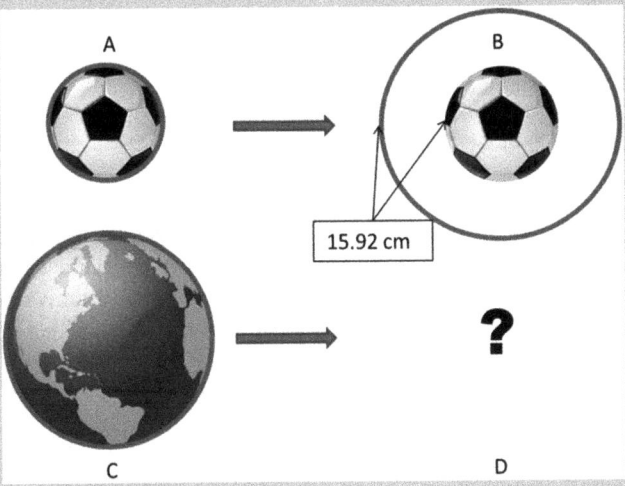

Fig. 2.1 Illustrating the pitfalls of intuition

The answer is yes, because the radius of the ball and the original circle is $70 \text{ cm}/2\pi = 11.14$ cm and the radius of the bigger circle is $170 \text{ cm}/2\pi = 27.06$ cm. The distance of the bigger circle from the surface of the ball is thus 27.06 cm – 11.14 cm = 15.92 cm. The mouse can easily run on the surface of the ball without touching the rope. Most people would answer this question intuitively correctly.

How about if we replace the soccer ball by the globe? The circumference of the globe is about 40,000,000 m. Let us span the rope around the globe (case C), and increase the length of the rope with 1 m as before. Make a circle with the new, longer rope around the globe as was done for the soccer ball (case D). Is there sufficient space under the rope for the mouse to run on the surface of the globe? The intuition says 'no', but the correct answer is 'yes'.

Let us span the rope around the globe, and increase the length of the rope with 1 m as before. Let us make a circle with the new extended rope around the globe as we did for the soccer ball. Is there sufficient space for the mouse to run on the surface of the globe without touching the rope? The radius of the globe is about 40,000,000 m/ 2π = 6366,197.7237 m and the radius of the bigger circle is about 40,000,001/ 2π = 6,366,197.8828 m. The difference is 6,366,197.8828 m − 6,366,197.7237 m = 15.92 cm, which is exactly the same as before. A little bit junior high school math tells us that the space for the mouse is independent of the length of the radius of the original circle. Surprised? The intuition failed us.

The following example demonstrates a case which people usually answer quickly—but incorrectly.

> **Example 2.2 Average Speed**
> A person is driving 45 km 30 km/h. How fast should she drive back, so that the average speed would be equal to 60 km/h?

Most people who provide an intuitive quick answer, would say 90 km/h. What do you think? The correct answer can be found in the appendix to this chapter.

There are many optical illusions, which produce counter-intuitive perceptions. The reader may consult the following list: List of optical illusions—Wikipedia. https://en.wikipedia.org/wiki/.

> **Example 2.3 The Ebbinghaus Illusion**
> One of the best-known optical illusions is the Ebbinghaus illusion (Fig. 2.2). It is an illusion of relative size perception. If a circle is surrounded by large circles, it appears (relatively) smaller, compared to the case where the circle is surrounded by small circles. In both cases the orange circles are exactly the same size (which can be objectively measured). Interestingly, the distance of the surrounding circles also plays a role! The Ebbinghaus illusion has a link to decision-making. In a later chapter we discuss the phenomenon that the decision environment (or context) matters. If your favorite choice is surrounded by poor choices versus other good choices, makes a difference. Unless we are aware of the illusion, we easily draw wrong conclusions. We may observe a similar effect, when people eat food from small versus large plates. People eat more from a large plate.
>
> (continued)

Example 2.3 (continued)

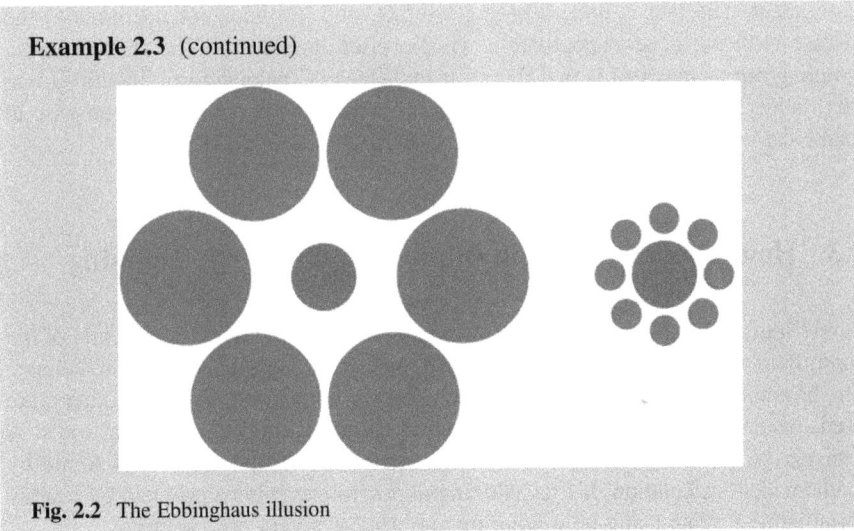

Fig. 2.2 The Ebbinghaus illusion

The two orange circles are exactly the same size; however, the one on the right appears larger. Taken from Wikipedia Commons.

Example 2.4 Understanding How New Information Influences Probabilities

The Economist published an article in the early 1990s at the height of the AIDS epidemic. The article was about a young person, who had committed suicide after finding out that (s)he had tested positive for the AIDS virus. At the time, there was no good medication. The article went further to analyze the situation and posed the following question: "Given a disease whose prevalence is 1:1000 and a diagnostics procedure (test), which errs in 5% of the cases, what is the probability that a patient who was diagnosed as being inflicted with the disease, actually has it?" Apparently, the figures reflected the situation at the time. The tests were in an early phase of development, hence the high 5% error rate. The same question was also presented to medical doctors, and many responded 95%. Those of you who have taken a class into probability, will quickly notice that an answer to the question can be calculated with the help of conditional probabilities. We do not discuss the correct solution here, but if you go through the math, the answer is about 2%! Intuition failed us. Intuition also sadly failed the young person in question, who committed suicide thinking that (s)he had AIDS. (Without additional tests, we do not know for sure, whether she had AIDS or not, but certainly the probability was not 0.95, but about 0.02.)

We return to this example in the chapter where we discuss biases with probability assessments. Just briefly, we think that two aspects in this example cloud our assessment. The first is understanding the fact, how common (or uncommon) the disease is in the general population. People often ignore this. The second aspect clouding our assessment is that the error rate (5%) of the diagnostic test (information) is awfully high in today's standards in medicine. It would have been wise to retake the test (For more details, see Moskowitz and Wright 1985).

2.3 How About Using Both Intuition and Analytic Thinking

Purely intuitive and purely analytic decision-making represent extreme ends of the continuum of decision-making styles. The purely intuitive style is based on feelings. The best choice is the one that the person feels to be the best. No other criteria are used. Instead, a purely analytic approach is based on the use of formal tools. A decision problem is presented in an exact form and the best solution is found by mathematical calculation. If it is natural and possible to solve a problem by exactly formulating it, then using pure intuition may lead to a very poor solution.

On the other hand, if you try to exactly solve such a decision problem, in which a decision maker's views, feelings, and preferences are modeled incorrectly, your solution is likely to be unsatisfactory. There are many problems, in which the best result is achieved by using a mixture of the extreme approaches (intuitive vs. analytic).

Appendix: Misleading Intuition

The one-way drive (45 km) with speed 30 km/h takes 90 min. A 90 km round-trip with average speed of 60 km/h takes 90 min. Hence there is zero time to return. Mathematically, the person would have to drive back infinitely fast.

References

Gigerenzer, G. (2008). *Gut feelings: The intelligence of the unconscious.* New York: Penguin Books.
Kahneman, D. (2011). *Thinking, fast and slow.* New York: Farrar, Straus, and Giroux.
List of Optical Illusions. *Wikipedia.* https://en.wikipedia.org/wiki/
Moskowitz, H., & Wright, G. (1985). *Statistics for management and economics.* Durham, NC: Bell & Howell.

Chapter 3
Towards Analytic Decision-Making

Our book is about decision-making and decision problems. 'Decision problem' refers to a situation in which we have to act (make a choice, decision) to find a way forward. We normally have several decision alternatives to choose from, sometimes just two, but often many. We may have just one criterion to judge the quality of decisions, but usually we have more than one criterion. Situations, which involve a decision problem, are very common.

The types of decision problems vary from simple to complex. As an example of a simple problem consider the following. It is late in the evening, and we are craving for some fruit. The only open grocery store is our small local store. Their choice of fruit is very limited (at this late hour). They basically have apples, oranges and bananas. Let us assume that we do not have a credit card with us, just one-euro coin. By looking at the fruits available in the store, we quickly realize that the apples are local (sour) Finnish apples, which we do not like. Moreover, the bananas have all started to rot. However, the oranges seem fine. We decide to buy oranges as many as our one-euro coin allows!

An example of a complex public-sector decision problem is, how much CO_2 emissions should be taxed? The answer depends on, how much CO_2 emissions influence global warming and how much global warming influences the economy. There are many features which make the problem complex:

1. The phenomena are so intertwined that it is extremely difficult to recognize all relevant causes and effects of different actions.
2. There is considerable uncertainty involved regarding the consequences of CO_2 emissions.
3. The problem is global, yet decisions are made at national levels.
4. There are several decision makers with different opinions.
5. Even though the government has expressed its common criteria, it is very plausible that the cabinet members have their own (hidden) criteria, which are not publicly revealed (not even to other cabinet members).

There are many complex problems, where all reasonable alternatives are not known. It is sometimes a good idea to brainstorm about creating alternatives.

3.1 Background

Managers need help in making decisions. Some managers realize this, some do not. Help could be needed in formulating the problem (alternatives). Alternatively, help could be needed in deciding what we want (our preferences). Corporate Linear Programming models existed already in the 1960s, with the purpose of aiding companies in their single-objective planning efforts. Decision support, as an academic field, developed during 1970s—and it has continued to develop ever since. Building upon giants' work (such as Abraham Charnes and William Cooper 1961), Decision Support Systems were pioneered by Michael Scott Morton (1971) and Keen and Scott Morton (1978). They published two influential books in the 1970s to set the stage for the field. Computers played an essential role in the evolving Decision Support Systems.

Our own involvement with computer-based decision support also began in the 1970s. Jyrki Wallenius, with Stanley Zionts, was actively developing interactive man-machine multi-criteria decision-making methods. Later the same decade, he began to collaborate with Pekka Korhonen. Their first research project concerned the development of a computer-based group Decision Support System.

In the 1970s many Operations Research scholars, including us, were fascinated about developing new decision algorithms and methods to aid decision-makers. It almost seemed that the algorithms and the methods became the focus instead of the problem, which the scholars wanted to solve. The 'hammer and nail' analogy seems fitting. We suppose it is tempting, if the only tool you have is a hammer, to treat everything as if it were a nail (Maslow 1966).

We, however, realized early on that we have better chances of supporting decision makers, if our models and tools are based on a sound behavioral foundation. Our book is about making wise choices, and helping decision makers choose wisely. This cannot be done properly without a discussion of behavioral decision issues. The late Ward Edwards is commonly referred to as the father of behavioral decision theory. He published two seminal articles, creating behavioral decision theory as a new field in psychology, one in 1954 and the other in 1961 (Edwards 1954, 1961). Another giant of behavioral decision-making was Herbert Simon, the Economics Nobel Laureate from 1978. In research published in mid-50s, he criticized the assumptions of the "rational man", and presented an alternative theory of choice, based on limited or bounded rationality (Simon 1955). In our book we also discuss the research of two other pioneers in the psychology of decision making, namely Amos Tversky and Daniel Kahneman. They collaborated over several decades, until the untimely death of Tversky in 1996. They published important work on the biases and heuristics of decision making, some of which is described in our book. In late 1970s they published an influential article titled "Prospect Theory" (Kahneman and Tversky 1979, which developed an alternative theory of choice to the classical model). Tversky and Kahneman studied the riskless version of prospect theory a decade later (Tversky and Kahneman 1991).

3.2 Fundamental Concepts

Many of our decisions are simple and can be made fast. For instance, when we drive a car and want to turn left, we take the left lane. We do not even realize that we have made a decision. Our experience has taught us, how to make necessary maneuvers safely. We have made the same decision many times before and learnt how to do it. No systematic analysis is needed.

Humans make many decisions without actually analyzing the problem, even if they have no experience on similar decision situations. They will make a choice, although they may not know why. They may have a "gut-feeling" that this is a good choice. Some decisions may even be "once in a life time"—type decisions. To most people the choice of the spouse is a typical example.

There are many ways to classify decision-making styles and decision problems. Typically, decision styles are classified into two classes: *intuitive versus analytic*. With the term "intuitive" we refer to decisions based on feelings rather than facts and proofs. Daniel Kahneman uses the terms System 1 and System 2, to refer to the intuitive vs. analytical approach (Kahneman 2011). We do not wish to imply that an intuition-based decision is necessarily worse than an analysis-based decision, although intuition has its limits. Sometimes the analytic approach is too heavy.

If the decision problem is highly complex, it is possible, in fact plausible that neither the analytic approach nor the intuitive approach leads to a good result. In both approaches, we have to simplify the problem into an understandable and/or solvable form, but the simplification entails a risk that essential features are lost. For instance, in the analytic approach it may happen that the "wrong" problem is solved exactly. Often, both approaches are needed. Some features of the problem can be systematically analyzed, others not.

Many decision problems, although not all, also have uncertainty about the future states, or both uncertainty and multiple criteria. Uncertainty is usually modelled with the help of probabilities. Although a fascinating subject, probabilities are not easy to estimate (subjectively) and they are subject to various biases. Our approach in this book about dealing with uncertainty is to use 'scenario thinking'. However, we do not seek to attach specific probabilities to different scenarios. Instead, we ask the decision-maker to process the uncertainty in her mind.

In this book, we focus on analytic decision-making in the presence of several criteria and refer to this kind of decision-making environment with the expression "*Multiple Criteria Decision Making*" (MCDM). In MCDM, the aim is to make rational decisions. The decision is rational if it is nondominated. Nondominated alternatives have the following property: there exists no other alternative having all criterion values at least as good as that of the chosen alternative and at least one criterion value better. Alternatives which are not nondominated, are dominated.

We will illustrate dominance with examples.

Example 3.1 Dominance
With Fig. 3.1 we illustrate a rational choice. It is about comparing apples and oranges.

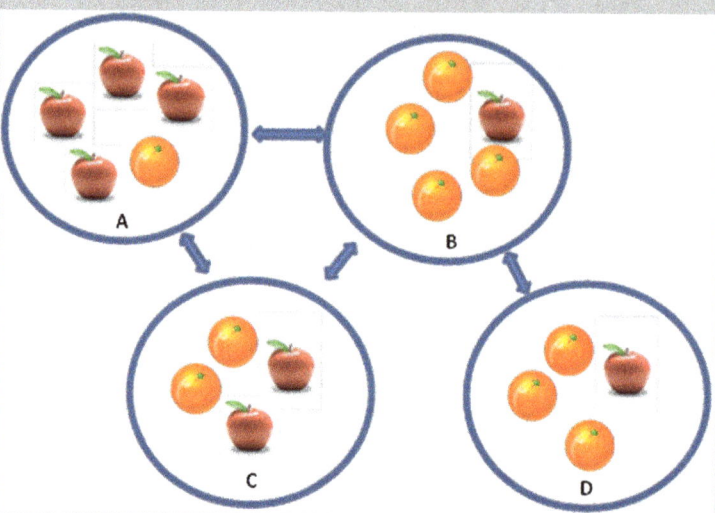

Fig. 3.1 Illustrative example about a multiple criteria decision-making problem

In Fig. 3.1, we have apples and oranges on four plates: A, B, C, and D. Our decision problem is to pick one plate. Assume that price is of no concern. All plates are free of charge. Assume that our criteria are 'to have as many oranges as possible' and 'to have as many apples as possible'. This is a bi-criteria problem. Unfortunately, there is not one ideal solution for the problem. Compromises are needed!

Which plate to choose? If we choose plate D, it is clearly not a rational choice. It is dominated. On plate B there is one more orange than on plate D; both plates have one apple. Instead, choosing any of the plates A, B, or C is a rational (or nondominated) choice. Which plate is chosen depends on our preference for apples and oranges (at the time of choosing). If we choose any of the plates A, B, or C, we cannot objectively argue that our decision was stupid.

If we like apples more than oranges, then plate A is a good choice; if we prefer oranges to apples, plate B sounds fine. A good compromise is plate C.

Example 3.1 illustrates the most important features of a Multiple Criteria Decision-Making problem:

- There is more than one criterion (in our case two: 'to have as many oranges as possible' and 'to have as many apples as possible')
- There are several nondominated alternatives (in our case, three plates), and
- The final choice should be one of the nondominated alternatives; it is based on the decision-maker's (DM) preferences.

Let us elaborate on each of these features in the following:

Criteria

How to approach an MCDM problem, heavily depends on the number and nature of criteria, which are used to judge the alternatives.

When the number of criteria is large, the DM presumably has difficulties to simultaneously evaluate the alternatives with all criteria. If the number of criteria is large, we may resort to visual representations. Luckily, however, when the number of criteria is large, the number of alternatives is small or reasonable. An example of a problem that has a large number of criteria and a small number of alternatives is the choice of the constructor for a new nuclear power plant. It is clear that this kind of problem is entirely different from buying a home in the Helsinki metropolitan area, where there are lots of (good) choices.

A criterion may be quantitative (presented in numeric form), or it may be qualitative. For a qualitative criterion we cannot provide a universal numerical scale. See Chap. 7 for an example of the use of qualitative criteria.

Alternatives

There is no one correct way to find, generate or represent alternatives. Our advice is that companies should spend time on making reasonably sure that they have identified (all) good alternatives. When a company hires a new employee, they usually advertise the open position. But it is important, in which outlets (web, media) the position has been advertised, or whether headhunters are used. Often the starting point is that all (good) alternatives are available and exist, and the decision is to select the best one using multiple criteria.[1] This type of problem is called *Multiple Criteria Evaluation* problem. Such problems typically have a finite number of alternatives.

There are other types of problems. For instance, when a company is looking for the best production plan for the next year, it typically considers various alternatives. In this case, the alternatives do not exist, but they must be designed. The term *Multiple Criteria Design* is used to refer to this type of problem. In theory, such problems have an infinite number of alternatives, and they are usually defined with mathematical constraints (inequalities). The set that fulfills all constraints, is the feasible set of decision alternatives. In Chap. 7 we discuss such problems.

---

[1] If the company is not satisfied with the current set of available candidates, we may have to continue the search. Such problems are discussed in Chap. 7.

Final Choice

When a DM chooses one alternative from the set of nondominated alternatives, which pleases her most, the choice is rational and represents the Most Preferred Solution (MPS). To find the MPS may not be easy. To compare nondominated alternatives with many criteria simultaneously makes the decision cognitively demanding. You gain in some of the criteria, and you lose in some. Such choices involve making tradeoffs (balancing) between conflicting criteria, which may be hard. The marketing literature talks about "tradeoff aversion", implying that humans do not like to make choices which involve tradeoffs. For example, if you desire a better-quality product, you generally must pay more for it.

Decision-Maker and Decision

We often assume that we know who the decision-maker is. We further assume that she is a single individual. In the real-world this may not be the case. Experts in an organization often prepare decisions. They then recommend a course of action for their boss. In this case, the boss may simply be a "titular or formal decision-maker", but the individuals who prepared the case, are in practice the actual decision-makers. In the public sector, it is fairly common that the decision-maker is a body or committee, who might vote for the best course of action. In the real-world, analysts may not have access to the actual decision-maker, but have to be content with working with the experts advising the decision-maker.

The decision theory literature does not necessarily have a good definition for a "decision". It is commonly referred to as the final choice (for implementation). Our colleague, Professor Ami Arbel, University of Tel-Aviv, defines a decision as an irreversible commitment of resources. One can naturally change the original decision, but according to this logic, by spending additional resources. We like this definition, but realize that the word "irreversible" may not always be clear.

3.3 Wise Decisions

When is a decision wise? The answer depends on the decision problem. If you buy a hat, and if you are happy with your decision, who can say that you made a bad choice. Perhaps your spouse has a different opinion. If she (or somebody else) makes you regret your purchase, maybe your decision cannot be regarded as very wise. But if you are constantly happy with your new hat, you have found for your own needs a solution, which pleases you. Your decision is wise.

Let us continue this example a bit longer. Assume that next door the exactly same hat is for sale with a clearly cheaper price. If you knew about this, then the decision is not wise (rational), provided there was no other reason (such as an attractive salesperson) to buy the hat in this specific store. If we do not know all the criteria the person has used in her choice, there is no objective way to claim that the choice is not wise (rational).

3.3 Wise Decisions

If a decision problem has a solution, which is objectively best (=correct), then the wrong choice is clearly not wise. We illustrate with two examples.

An example of a choice, which is not wise, is plate D (dominated by B) in Fig. 3.1 Plates B and D both have one apple, but plate B has one orange more than plate D.

Example 3.2 Track and Field
Consider a 10-k run on a stadium. It is run on a 400 m long track. The track has two semi-circles, which are connected with straight lines. It is important to know the width of the lane ($\Delta r = 122$ cm) (International Association of Athletics Federations, IAAF). If an athlete runs one semi-circle on the second lane, (s)he will run 3.83 m ($=2\pi \cdot 1.22/2$) more than an athlete on the inner lane. If the athlete runs all the time on the second lane, s(he) runs 50 semi-circles, which means s(he) runs 191.5 m more than a wise athlete using the inner lane. The Finnish running legend of the 1920s, Paavo Nurmi, knew this intuitively, and would always, if possible, use the inner-most lane.

The following example demonstrates that it matters which criteria we use in decision-making. Nondominance is defined via criteria, and so is 'wiseness'.

Example 3.3 Criteria Matter
Assume that five students have passed a number of different courses and received a non-excellent or an excellent grade from each course (see Table 3.1). Assume that we want to reward the 'best' student with a scholarship. How do we go about finding the 'best student' based on this information?

Table 3.1 Excellent, non-excellent and total sum of grades of five students

Students	Criteria		
	EG	NEG	TG = EG + NEG
A	10	0	10
B	10	1	11
C	9	3	12
D	8	4	12
E	6	5	11

It sounds quite natural to use as criteria 'the number of excellent grades (EG)' and 'the number of non-excellent, but acceptable grades (NEG)', which the student has accumulated. Without losing any information, we may replace the criterion NEG by the criterion 'the number of total grades (TG)', which is the sum of excellent and non-excellent (acceptable) grades.

Let us consider the use of the criteria EG and TG. We may make the following observations: B is better than A, because B and A have the same

(continued)

> **Example 3.3** (continued)
> number of excellent grades, but in addition B has one total grade more. C is better than D, because it has one excellent grade more and the number of total grades is the same. B and C are both better than E. Thus, we can eliminate students A, D, and E. The best student is either B or C. Which one is chosen depends on the judge's preferences. If the number of excellent grades is preferred to the number of total grades, then the choice is B; otherwise C. In both cases, the decision is wise.
>
> If we use EG and NEG as the criteria, and focus on nondominance, the outcome changes. Student A can be rejected as before, but all other students are nondominated. However, why to choose D instead of C, or E instead of B? D and E are nondominated, but choosing them can be criticized, because we prefer an excellent grade to a non-excellent grade. It is not wise to choose either D or E. Criteria matter!

3.4 Dangers of Oversimplification

Consider the following simple example.

> **Example 3.4 Curse of Mediocrity**
> The manager of a company would like to hire a new secretary. Assume that she has interviewed candidates, and picked three best ones. The candidates are quite similar, but the most discriminating features are 'IT knowledge' and 'Work history'. The manager decides to use a "scientific" approach for the final choice. She gives the scores 1–10 (10 is best) for all candidates on both criteria. A has an excellent work history (score 10), but (s)he has very poor knowledge of IT (score 1); B's work history is not impressive (score 1), but (s)he has excellent IT knowledge (10). Candidate C has a fair work history (score 5) and fair knowledge in IT (score 5). The situation is described in Fig. 3.2.
>
> Assume that the manager thinks that work history and IT knowledge are equally important, and she decides to use the weighted sum (with equal weights) to be able to rank the candidates. The blue line describes equally preferred points. The result is that A and B are equally good, but C will never be chosen, even if the weights of the scores are varied. The manager is hardly happy, because C is reasonably good on both criteria! Perhaps it is unwise to use an exact method (weighted scores) for this choice problem. Or you could perhaps think out of the box, and hire both A and B.

3.5 Wrapping up

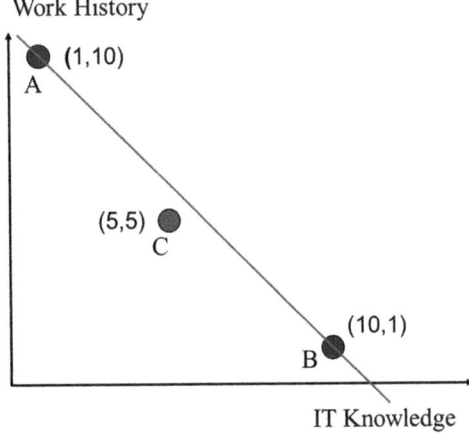

Fig. 3.2 Graphical representation of the scores of three job candidates

3.5 Wrapping up

Sometimes a person appears to choose a seemingly unwise, dominated alternative. Think about a recruiting situation, where the boss chooses a person, who is worse than the other applicants in terms of educational background, intelligence, work experience, etc. (the explicit criteria). However, the person chosen happens to be the nephew of the boss. She simply wanted to help her nephew (a hidden criterion). Hence the choice in our terminology is wise (given that the nephew does not have too large responsibilities, and will not cause damage to the company). Our advice is always to try to list and make explicit all relevant criteria.

Many of us have attended internal meetings, where someone has advocated an alternative, which is dominated when judged with the criteria articulated in the meeting. In such a case, it is good to think, what hidden criteria the person has—assuming that the person is not stupid (which is seldom the case).

In this chapter we have described three different types of wise decisions:

- The decision criteria are not explicitly stated, because they are not even conscious or the decision-maker does not want to make them explicit. In this case a wise decision is any decision, which pleases the decision-maker most.
- The outcome of a decision can be measured with one or several criteria and the best solution can be mathematically calculated. Then a wise decision is the mathematically optimal or correct solution.
- The decision problem is an MCDM problem, where all the criteria are known. If we have no information about the decision-maker's preferences, then choosing any nondominated alternative is a wise decision.[2]

---

[2]Sometimes we have preference restrictions, which can be 'common sense' restrictions, such as in Example 3.3 'excellent' grades are preferred to 'good' grades. Such information should naturally be considered.

References

Charnes, A., & Cooper, W. W. (1961). *Management models and industrial applications of linear programming*. New York: Wiley.
Edwards, W. (1954). The theory of decision making. *Psychological Bulletin, 51*(4), 380–417.
Edwards, W. (1961). Behavioral decision theory. *Annual Review of Psychology, 12*, 473–498.
Kahneman, D. (2011). *Thinking, fast and slow*. New York: Farrar, Straus, and Giroux.
Kahneman, D., & Tversky, A. (1979). Prospect theory: An analysis of decision under risk. *Econometrica, 47*, 262–291.
Keen, P. G. W., & Scott Morton, M. S. (1978). *Decision support systems: An organizational perspective*. Reading, MA: Addison-Wesley.
Maslow, A. (1966). *The psychology of science: A reconnaissance*. Chicago: Chicago Gateway.
Scott Morton, M. S. (1971). *Management decision systems: Computer-based support for decision making*. Boston: Division of Research, Graduate School of Business Administration, Harvard University.
Simon, H. (1955). A behavioral model of rational choice. *Quarterly Journal of Economics, 69*, 99–118.
Tversky, A., & Kahneman, D. (1991). Loss aversion in riskless choice: A reference-dependent model. *Quarterly Journal of Economics, 106*(4), 1039–1061.

Chapter 4
How Do Humans Make Choices?

Humans have been making decisions for tens of thousands of years. Over the years they have developed different 'ways' of making decisions. Scholars have developed theories to model human decision-making based on each 'way' of making decisions. In this chapter we discuss the pros and cons of several commonly used ways of making decisions. They have been found useful, although they also have their limitations. We discuss the satisficing approach and contrast it with the optimizing approach, the lexicographic model, the compensatory models, 'Elimination By Aspects'-model, and prospect theory.

Although the focus of our book is in supporting decision-makers, we feel that it is important for us to understand how humans make decisions. The better we understand this, the better are our chances to support decision-makers. Hence we want to devote a chapter to how humans make choices.

4.1 Satisficers

Herbert Simon introduced the concept of limited or bounded rationality already in mid-50s (Simon 1955). He strongly argued that humans do not have the cognitive and computational capacity for making 'optimal' decisions. Instead, according to him, the human rationality is bounded or limited. Accordingly, humans are more prone to satisficing behavior. If you find a satisficing alternative, say a hat that you like, you go ahead and buy it. You do not go into the trouble of visiting all the hat stores in your city to make sure that you have found the best possible hat in the market. Whether you are more a satisficer or an optimizer, is personal. Some people are more prone to being satisficers than optimizers.[1]

A more formal way to look at the satisficing model is to set aspiration levels (or targets) for all your decision-relevant criteria. As soon as you find an alternative, which meets all your aspiration levels, you stop. You have found a satisficing alternative.

4.2 Lexicographic Model

The name of this model comes from 'lexicon', which arranges words alphabetically starting with *a*. Words starting with *a* are organized according to the second letter, and so forth. If we use this model in decision-making, we arrange the criteria in terms of importance. The origins of the lexicographic model are old and a bit fuzzy.

> **Example 4.1 Hiring an Employee**
> Table 4.1 refers to the problem of hiring an employee. The rows refer to applicants and the columns to criteria. The columns have been arranged so that the most important column is the left-most (Education), the second most important criterion (Work Experience) corresponds to the second column, and the third column corresponds to the third most important criterion (Computing Skills). Regarding education, 3 refers to master's degree, 2 to bachelor's degree, and 1 to high school diploma (the higher the degree, the better). Regarding work experience, the numbers refer to years of relevant work experience (again, the more the better). Regarding computing skills, we have classified the applicant pool to three classes: 3 means excellent computing skills (relevant from the point of view of the job), 2 good skills, and 1 minimal skills.
>
> **Table 4.1** Illustrating the lexicographic model
>
> | | Education | Work experience | Computing skills |
> |-------------|-----------|-----------------|------------------|
> | Applicant A | 2 | 8 | 2 |
> | Applicant B | 2 | 6 | 3 |
> | Applicant C | 1 | 15 | 3 |
> | Applicant D | 1 | 18 | 1 |

---

[1] Interestingly, one could argue that the satisficers are optimizers with a rather large search cost. If you incorporate the search cost into the model, there is not such a large difference between optimizers and satisficers.

We first look at the most important criterion and compare applicants regarding education. Applicants A and B have a bachelor's degree, but the other two only a high school diploma. Hence, based on the lexicographic model, we eliminate applicants C and D from further consideration. Applicants A and B are tied in terms of the most important criterion. The lexicographic model then tells us to look at the second most important criterion (Work Experience), but only considering applicants A and B. Applicant A has 8 years of work experience and applicant B 6 years. Since more years of work experience is better, we should choose applicant A. The third criterion (Computing Skills) plays no role. It does not help applicant B that her Computing Skills are better than applicant A's.

What is typical about the lexicographic model is that poor (or even slightly poorer) values in the most important criterion (criteria) cannot be compensated by other criteria, no matter how good they are. That is why the lexicographic model is a so called non-compensatory model.

Is this a good model? When can or should it be used? Let us say that the lexicographic model is rather specific. It is applicable, but in rather specific circumstances. Some problems do possess the most important criterion. But it is rather rare that all other criteria could be arranged in their order of importance. Think about aircraft design. The most important criterion is (at least should be) passenger and crew safety. But it is less clear, how the companies rank the other design criteria, and there may also be tradeoffs involved. Safer designs may very well be more expensive.

Decision-makers typically can rank criteria in terms of importance. However, it is often not clear what they mean by such importance rankings. We revisit this issue later in our book.

4.3 Compensatory Models

Compensatory models have the property that poor(er) values in some criteria may be compensated by good (better) values in other criteria. No importance ranking for criteria is needed. A typical weighting model is a case in point. Weighting models or scoring models are commonly used by managers. The general (mis)belief is that the weights would reflect importance. Let us try to solve Example 4.1 with weights. Let us assume that our decision maker has thought hard about the 'importance weights' and feels comfortable with weights 0.6 for Education, 0.25 for Work Experience, and 0.15 for Computing Skills. If we multiply the values of each row in the table with these weights, a simple arithmetic calculation tells us that applicant D is best (with a weighted sum of 5.25), applicant C the second best (4.8), followed by applicant A (3.5) and applicant B (3.15). Are you happy with this? The weights supposedly reflect the 'order of importance'. The most important criterion has the largest weight, the second most important criterion has the second largest weight, and so on.

There are two problems with this weighting approach. Firstly, the scales in which the criterion values have been expressed, matter. They in fact go hand in hand with the weights. It is not enough to scale the weights so that they add up to 1. Perhaps we should scale the values so that for each criterion the best value gets the score equal to 100 and the worst 0, and the remaining values are in-between. If you undergo the arithmetic with the new scale, the winner is B (with weighted sum equal to 83.3). The second best is A (with a score equal to 78.6).

Even if we properly scale the criterion values, the second problem remains. Namely, how to determine the weights? We have a suggestion, which we will discuss at length in a later chapter.

4.4 Elimination by Aspects

Tversky presented the Elimination By Aspects model in a psychology journal in 1972. It was a descriptive model of choice, in other words reflecting (in his opinion) how human people make choices. The idea is simple and appealing, although the article itself is hard reading. This theory is based on an elimination process, in which each alternative is viewed as a set of aspects. All alternatives which do not possess the aspect, are eliminated. We progress one aspect at a time, until we have eliminated all but one alternative. We illustrate with an example.

> **Example 4.2 Buying a Car**
> Let us consider buying a new car (instead of a used car). Different cars (on the market) have different features (which Tversky calls aspects), such as make (Honda, Mercedes, Toyota), model (Honda Accord, Honda CRV), the luxury version or basic version, size of engine, price, color, 4-door vs. 2-door sedans vs. SUV^{2}s, and so forth. Let us now think about how you would go about buying a car using the Elimination By Aspects model. First you must think of the most important aspect that you want in the car. Perhaps it is price, and accordingly you may set a price range, say 25,000–30,000 euros. Using price, we would eliminate all cars which are either less expensive than 25,000 euros or more expensive than 30,000 euros. This narrows down the search, although there are still plenty of cars in that price range.
>
> Next, let us assume that we have previously had a Japanese car, which we thought was good value for money. Accordingly, we limit ourselves to Japanese cars (in the price range 25,000–30,000 euros). This will considerably limit the available choices. The next important aspect of the car is that it is large enough for the family (and luggage), hence we consider it important that
>
> (continued)

---

[2]Sport Utility Vehicle.

Example 4.2 (continued)
it is an SUV. Now we have limited ourselves to buying a car in the price range 25,000–30,000 euros, which is a Japanese SUV. The Japanese car manufacturers each typically have an SUV (Honda's SUV is called CRV; Toyota's SUV is RAV, Nissan's SUV is Qashqai). Our neighbor has a Honda CRV and he says it is a great car. We follow his advice, and will focus on Honda CRVs. We still need to decide whether we want the basic model or a more expensive enhanced version (naturally automatic), and the color. And then we visit some local Honda dealers and start negotiating! And hopefully end up buying a car.

Tversky suggests that humans typically conduct the elimination starting with the most important aspect(s). Despite its natural appeal, Elimination By Aspects model is sensitive to the order in which the elimination process is carried out. The order of eliminating aspects resembles the lexicographic model. We think it is a good question, whether humans can reliably establish such an order of elimination. It is also quite plausible that as a result of the elimination process, we have no alternatives left. In that case we should revisit some of the aspects (in our example, probably the price).

Next, let us revisit Example 4.1: Hiring an Employee. Let us try two different orders of elimination. The first going from left to right, and the second going from right to left. Let us first consider going from left to right. Let us eliminate all alternatives whose values are below 2 in the first column, leaving us with A and B. Using the second aspect (criterion) to eliminate applicants with values below 7, we are left with A. Going from right to left, excluding options with values below 3 in Computing Skills eliminates A and D (B and C left). Eliminating options below 7 (Work Experience) will eliminate B (C left). If you stop the process when you have one option left, you end up with A in the first case, and C in the second case!

4.5 Prospect Theory or the Reference-Dependent Model

Prospect theory due to Kahneman and Tversky (1979) is probably the most celebrated theory of choice of the latter half of the twentieth century. Kahneman received the Nobel Prize in Economics in 2002, in part, for his and Tversky's work on prospect theory. Prospect theory is a descriptive theory of choice for decisions under uncertainty, but the theory (parts of it) is very relevant for riskless choice (Korhonen et al. 1990; Tversky and Kahneman 1991). We review the essential aspects of the theory, which are relevant for our purposes.

There are a couple of essential aspects, which differentiate prospect theory from other theories of choice. Firstly, according to prospect theory, humans normally evaluate alternatives with respect to a reference point. In other words, they are more accustomed to judging relative rather than absolute quantities. Tversky and Kahneman are a bit vague regarding, what reference points people use. Typical reference points are status-quo or expected state of affairs. We illustrate with a simple example.

> **Example 4.3 Labor-Management Negotiations**
> Imagine labor-management negotiations about salary increases for workers for next year. Let us assume that the workers have been promised a 5% increase in their salaries. Before the contract is signed, the boss from the employer's side is fired, and a new guy replaces him. She is aware of the previous promise, but thinks the employer cannot afford a 5% salary increase for workers. Instead she offers 3%. Not surprisingly, the workers and their representatives are outraged. They do not consider 3% as +3%, but rather −2% (from the promised 5%). The expected (promised) 5% had become the reference point, against which the new offer was judged. Values above the reference point are called gains, values below it losses. It should not come as a surprise if a strike followed.

Besides the reference point, another specific feature of prospect theory is that humans typically react more strongly to negative stimuli (losses) than positive stimuli (gains). In other words, if we give 20 euros to somebody, she is happy and her utility increases by, say A (A is subjective and its size does not matter). If we instead force (or trick) her to pay us 20 euros, she is clearly upset, since her utility has decreased (compared to the no-payment situation) by clearly more than A. This phenomenon is generally called loss aversion. Moreover, according to Kahneman and Tversky, people are generally risk averse for gains and risk prone for losses. Most people are risk averse for moderate and large amounts of money (what is large, is again, personal); interestingly, according to prospect theory they are risk prone for losses. They are willing to gamble to avoid incurring losses. Of course, they could lose more!

In prospect theory the preference between negative outcomes is the mirror image of the preference between positive outcomes. This phenomenon is called the reflection effect. In other words, it is not uncommon that a person prefers say 3000 euros for certain to a 0.8 probability of winning 4000 euros (the probability of winning nothing is 0.2). However, people with this preference structure commonly prefer losing 4000 euros with probability 0.8 (again, there is a 0.2 probability of not losing at all) to a certain loss of 3000.

We like prospect theory and its riskless version. However, it is important to realize that it was intended as a descriptive model of choice, how people behave. It was not meant as a normative model to use as a guideline, how people should behave. Also, as a descriptive model it is not really an operational model. To operationalize it, we would need to find out what reference points people use. In our own research we have used the current solution (status-quo) as the reference point. The reference point plays a key role in the theory.

Psychologists have criticized prospect theory for lack of psychological explanations for the in-built processes. Factors that are of great importance to decision-making processes, such as emotions, have not been included in the model.

4.6 Evidence for Prospect Theory or the Riskless Version

Colin Camerer (2000) in his article "Prospect Theory in the Wild" describes real world evidence for prospect theory. In total, he describes ten cases which according to him support prospect theory. Although some of the cases have generated a debate, and alternative explanations for the underlying phenomena have been offered, we briefly describe six of the cases. Camerer explains all these six phenomena with loss aversion or the reflection effect.

1. Holding losing stocks too long, selling winning stocks too early. Does this sound familiar? Anyone inherited stock that you kept a way too long? The prospect theory explanation is that humans typically quickly update their reference point in bull markets, but do not behave this way in bear markets. In other words, humans do not necessarily believe that the market is declining, and hence they do not as frequently update the reference point in bear markets.
2. Downward sloping labor supply: particularly inexperienced New York City cab drivers said they set an income target for each day and quit when the target was reached. The implication is that the drivers work long days when demand is slow, and work shorter days (at least not longer days), when demand is high. The daily income target forms a reference point. Drivers hate to fall short, but are not very enthusiastic to exceed the target either.
3. Purchases are more sensitive to price increases than to cuts. Price increases are losses, and people are more sensitive to them than to corresponding gains.[3]
4. When people's income was expected to rise, people tended to spend more. However, consumers do not necessarily cut consumption after receiving bad income news, as standard economic theory predicts. Insensitivity to bad news is explained with the help of loss aversion.
5. Status quo bias: people have an exaggerated preference for the status quo, or the default option. For example, consumers do not switch health plans, even if it were in their interest, but choose default health insurance. In prospect theory language, status quo or default option is a powerful reference point. Probably some aspects

---

[3]One of our former Ph.D. students, Outi Somervuori studied this phenomenon in detail in her dissertation (Somervuori 2012). According to her, behavior around the reference point may not only be loss aversive but also gain seeking and symmetric, showing that the problem is more complicated than originally thought.

Fig. 4.1 Prospect theory value function

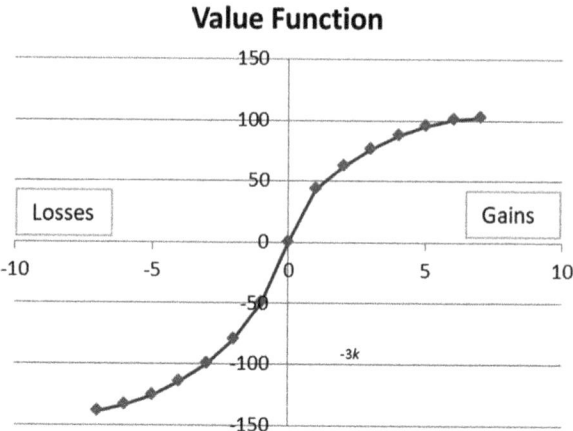

in the alternative plans are worse than in the status quo. According to prospect theory, people hate such losses and overweigh them.

6. End-of-the-day effect: in horse race betting, people shift to long shots at the end of the day.[4] The effect has traditionally been explained by risk prone behavior. A more plausible explanation is prospect theory. People hate to go home (at the end of the day) and admit that they lost. By long shots they try to recover the money lost during the day. The explanation is reflection effect.

Appendix: More Details on Prospect Theory

In decision making, the concept of a value function is used to measure the value of money (or other attributes). On the x-axis is money, and on the y-axis the value of different amounts of money. Normally a value function (the x-axis) would start from zero and be increasing. In other words, the more money we have, the better.

Prospect theory value function covers (on the x-axis) both positive (gains) and negative (losses) amounts. We illustrate a typical prospect theory value function in Fig. 4.1. In technical jargon, the value function is concave for gains and convex for losses. It is also steeper for same sized losses than gains, implying that people react more strongly to negative than positive stimuli (loss aversion).

---

[4]In horse racing, long shots are bets with a relatively small chance of winning. However, if a long shot wins, the payoff is considerable.

Where We Have Used Prospect Theory

In our research (Korhonen et al. 1990), we observed 'strange' behavior by human subjects, who were making choices comparing washing machines against other washing machines and homes against other homes in the Helsinki metro-area. We noticed that they sometimes made loops (or cycles), in other words returned to a previously discarded alternative. They also rather frequently abruptly (or prematurely) stopped the search for better alternatives. We showed that the riskless version of prospect theory could be used to explain both phenomena. We also noticed that so-called path dependence is a direct consequence of the riskless version of prospect theory. We explain below all these three phenomena.

Cycles

Assume that you are comparing two houses, house A and house B. Let us assume that house A is your reference house (your current home). When comparing A against B, we notice that some of the criterion values (perhaps location or condition, or yard) are worse in B than in A. We experience the (negative) difference in criterion values as losses, and react strongly to them; even though some of the criterion values in B are better than in A, we anyway reject B.

Now think that for some reason house B is your reference point (it is perhaps your wife's old childhood home that she really loves), and you repeat the comparison. Again, some of criterion values in A are worse than in B, and in the overall judgment we reject A because of the loss aversion phenomenon! In a nutshell, if A is your reference point, it is preferred to B. However, if B is your reference point, then it is preferred to A.

Premature Stopping

When we consider nondominated alternatives and compare them against each other, some of the criterion values are better and some worse. According to the riskless version of prospect theory, people overweigh the losses, and are not willing to accept such trades. As a consequence, they stop, perhaps sooner than they should. We call this phenomenon tradeoff aversion.

Path Dependence

In classical optimization (where no human is involved), it does not matter what you use as the starting point for the optimization algorithm. We will find the optimal solution, irrespective of the starting point.

When humans are involved in the decision process, things are not necessarily as simple any more. The starting point, and generally the path which we travel towards the Most Preferred Solution, impacts where we end up. The explanation offered is the riskless version of prospect theory. The assumption is that we update our reference point to be the Most Preferred Solution so far found. As we have seen, the reference point has an impact on where we end up.

References

Camerer, C. (2000). Prospect theory in the wild – Evidence from the field. In D. Kahneman & A. Tversky (Eds.), *Choices, values, and frames* (pp. 288–300). Cambridge: Cambridge University Press.

Kahneman, D., & Tversky, A. (1979). Prospect theory: An analysis of decision under risk. *Econometrica, 47*(2), 263–292.

Korhonen, P., Moskowitz, H., & Wallenius, J. (1990). Choice behavior in interactive multiple criteria decision making. *Annals of Operations Research, 23*(1), 161–179.

Simon, H. (1955). A behavioral model of rational choice. *The Quarterly Journal of Economics, 69*(1), 99–118.

Somervuori, O. (2012). *Essays on behavioral pricing*. Doctoral Dissertations 124/2012, Aalto University Publication Series.

Tversky, A. (1972). Elimination by aspects: A theory of choice. *Psychological Review, 79*(4), 281–299.

Tversky, A., & Kahneman, D. (1991). Loss aversion in riskless choice: A reference-dependent model. *Quarterly Journal of Economics, 106*(4), 1039–1061.

Chapter 5
Beware of Decision Traps: The World of Certainty

We quote Hammond, Keeney, and Raiffa's *Harvard Business Review* paper from 1998: "So where do bad decisions come from? In many cases, they can be traced back to the way the decisions were made—the alternatives were not clearly defined, the right information was not collected, the costs and benefits were not accurately weighed. But sometimes the fault lies not in the decision-making process but rather in the mind of the decision-maker. The way the human brain works can sabotage our decisions."

When facing complex decisions, we often use simplifying heuristics. Such heuristics have been studied by prominent psychologists, notably by Amos Tversky and Daniel Kahneman. Their article published in Science in 1974 is a classic. The heuristics often work to our advantage in simplifying complicated situations. However, a word of caution is in order. The use of simplifying heuristics is a cause of many bad decisions. Following other scholars, we call them decision traps (Russo and Schoemaker 1989). We should be aware of them. And we should try to guard us against them: 'forewarned is forearmed'.

5.1 Hearing What You Want to Hear

We believe that the confirming evidence trap is one of the most serious and common traps in the corporate world. The term is almost self-explanatory. There are two underlying psychological forces which can explain it. The first is the natural human tendency to subconsciously decide what we want to do or to achieve before we figure out, why we want to do it. The second is the human tendency to do things we are fond of rather than things we do not like. It is easier to surround oneself by like-minded people than dissidents or opponents. These two underlying psychological forces explain our habit to listen to and gather advice supporting our original idea. Even big and successful corporate bosses are guilty of this. To make matters worse, corporate leaders are often hired because of their vision regarding which direction the company should develop. If the vision and the subsequent actions turn out to be good, everybody is happy. However, predominantly focusing on information supporting one's original idea is risky—and unnecessary. At worst, the confirming evidence bias manifests itself in hiring people we know will support our idea.

What to do about the confirming evidence trap? As we have previously discussed, we think that all people in leadership positions should use the devil's advocate approach. They should listen to people who can challenge and test the original vision. Important corporate decisions should all be subjected to a feasibility test.

For example, typically in construction projects costs are exceeded and deadlines are not met. The recent Helsinki Metropolitan Area west-bound subway project is a case in point. The costs exceeded the original estimates by some 38%, and the completion of the project was 1.5 years delayed from estimates conducted 3–4 years prior, according to a study by Ernest and Young. One should not surround her- or himself by yes-men and -women. Leaders need close advisors who are brilliant and have their own mind, who are capable and willing of challenging the leader. A case in point was President Kennedy's choice of his closest advisors and cabinet members. Several of them were Republicans, some corporate leaders, some academics. It is also important for the leader not to ask leading questions, additionally biasing the advisors.

5.2 Too Much Simplification

Myopic problem representation bias occurs, when an overly simplified problem representation is used based on an incomplete "mental model" of the problem. Myopic representation is typically manifested by concentrating on a small number of alternatives and a small number of objectives; possibly also a single future state. If a small number of alternatives and objectives is all that you need (and you are sure about this), then no problem. Simple is good, but not too simple, paraphrasing the famous quote by Einstein.

The key is that the problem representation should not miss on important aspects or dimensions of the problem. We give two examples. Firstly, think of a retail company which is rethinking prices for its products. If they solely base their decisions on their own cost and revenue structure, this is an example of a myopic problem representation. It would be naïve to assume that the competitors would not react. A price war might even result, depending on how aggressive our decisions are. Secondly, it is very risky for companies to ignore the impact of their decisions on environment or sustainable development. A recent example from Finland is the mining company Talvivaara, which ran into financial difficulties and is now operated under a new company named Terrafame. Talvivaara ignored the environment. In fact, The Dow Jones Sustainability Indices (DJSI), a family of indices evaluating how well companies trading publicly do sustainability-wise, were launched already in 1999. They are gaining in momentum. Other stock exchanges have adopted similar indices.

Advice on proper problem representation can be found in the academic literature (Montibeller and Von Winterfeldt 2015; Rosenhead 2013).

5.3 Context Matters

Context manifests itself in two possible ways. The first refers to the decision alternatives, which you have seen before making your decision (background context). The second refers to the set of decision alternatives which you are actively considering, when making the decision (local context) (Tversky and Simonson 1993). We illustrate both cases.

There is evidence that previously seen alternatives matter. We illustrate with a case involving one of the authors (Wallenius). Hannele and Jyrki Wallenius wanted to buy a condominium in Scottsdale, Arizona.

> **Example 5.1 Buying a Condo in Scottsdale, Arizona**
> During a spring morning, our realtor showed us many condos, which we did not like. Either the price-quality ratio was not right, or the neighborhood or unit's condition were poor. To make a long story short, when we expressed frustration about the condos shown to us, our realtor said that now she knows what we want. She showed us a brand-new condo area in North-Central Scottsdale, surrounded by beautiful golf courses. Immediately, after seeing a model condo for display (beautifully furnished), we said, we want this—and we stopped the search. The price-quality ratio was much better than in the previously seen units. We have been happy with the condo. However, in retrospect we could have continued the search and not taken the first decent one. Perhaps we could have considered a bit more upscale or bigger unit. We did not think long-term!

There is also evidence that the local context, that is the alternatives currently under consideration, matter. For example, alternatives with extreme values (within a set) appear less attractive than alternatives which have intermediate values. Also, by introducing a third alternative, one can influence the relative attractiveness of the two original decision alternatives. The alternatives may be products on display in brick-and-mortar stores or online shops; or political candidates running for office. In a nutshell, the same product (candidate) appears attractive against a background of less attractive products (candidates) and vice versa. Practical advice: do not go to a bar with a friend who is more handsome and attractive than you! The phenomenon is the same as the physical observation that a small circle surrounded by larger circles appears even smaller; and that a small circle surrounded by smaller circles appears larger (Ebbinghaus illusion).

Fig. 5.1 Effect of decoys

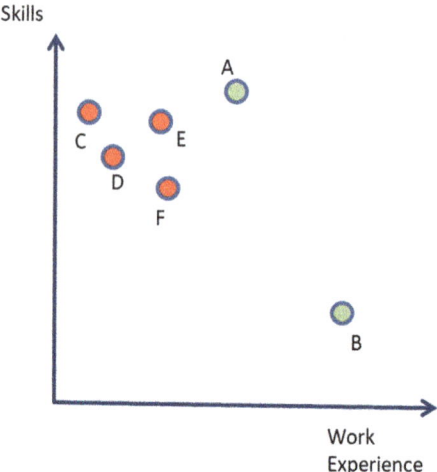

Use of Decoys

There are decision situations, in which advisers to a decision-maker are tempted to promote an alternative by means of a decoy. This may be true also about the decision-maker herself. We explain what we mean. A typical case is to create extra alternatives, which emphasize the superiority of an alternative, which somebody is trying to promote.

Assume that you are selecting a new employee for your company. Of course, you normally evaluate candidates with many criteria, but to make a point we simplify the situation by using only two criteria: *IT Skills* and *Work Experience*. Suppose that we have received six applications for the open job. As we can see from Fig. 5.1, the choice is, in principle, easy, because the actual choice is between the only two nondominated applicants: A or B. Alternative A dominates alternatives C, D, E, and F, i.e. is better on both criteria, but it does not dominate B.

If only candidates A and B were available, it is quite reasonable that the decision-maker might select candidate B, because of her larger work experience. However, in the situation described in Fig. 5.1, she will likely choose A. Why would she do that? The superiority of candidate A is emphasized in comparison with C, D, E, and F, whom A beats on both criteria. The underlying thinking is that since A is superior to four other alternatives, it must be good. Candidates C, D, E, and F are referred to as decoy alternatives. They may be candidates asked to apply for the job. Again, to combat the decoy bias, forewarned is forearmed.

5.4 Anchoring

The phenomenon of anchoring has been documented in hundreds of experiments. The anchor can be a past event (historical anchor), a trend, a story in the newspaper, first impression of a job applicant, basically anything that catches our eye. Often an anchor is a number. In prediction and in decision making, the anchor biases our estimates and decisions by receiving too much weight. People do realize that they cannot base estimates/decisions on anchors, hence they deviate from them. The problem is that the deviations are usually not large enough.

We illustrate with several examples. When asked about the sales forecasts for next year, the department heads often anchor on this year's sales. If the market is good, they might add 10%. If the market is declining, they might deduct 5%. The bottom line is that this year's sales may not be a good figure to base next year's sales figures on. The use of a longer history (trend) could be more reliable. The problem, however, with trends is that they are fine if nothing dramatic happens and things continue pretty much the way they have in the past several years. However, trends are not good in predicting recessions! They are no good in turbulent times.

In job interviews first impressions can be powerful anchors. The job applicants should know that this is the case, and make their best effort in presenting themselves well in the interview. There are consultants who provide advice even on what to wear to job interviews. However, the recruiting officer should perhaps not anchor on the first impression.

Aggressive negotiators often start with low-ball offers, with the hope that the other party would get discouraged and anchor on the low-ball initial offer. You should respond in the same aggressive way and show that you are not intimidated by the other party—and that you will not use their low-ball offer as the base for the negotiations.

It is a good idea to view a problem from different perspectives. Also, one should be open minded and seek information and opinions from a number of people. As with any of the biases and hidden decision traps, forewarned is forearmed. It already helps, if we are aware of the possibility of anchoring. Moreover, be careful not to anchor your advisers, and others from whom you solicit counsel. Hence it is a good idea for the boss to express her views after the others have spoken.

The Status-Quo Is Safer

There are strong forces at play, why people often anchor on the status-quo. To deviate from the status-quo is often risky. It means that we have to act. It somehow feels safer to stick to the status-quo. Why would I deviate from the status-quo, if my (smart) predecessors found it a good strategy? It is not uncommon to hear someone say: "let us not rock the boat, let us wait and see how the situation develops".

The status-quo may very well be your best choice. However, do not choose it just because it represents a comfortable choice. It should be a carefully thought out decision, if we stick to the status-quo. Hammond, Keeney, and Raiffa (1998) offer useful pieces of advice to avoid falling for the status-quo trap. They include the following:

- Never think of the status quo as your only alternative. Identify other options.
- Ask yourself whether you would choose the status-quo alternative, if it were not the status quo.
- Avoid exaggerating the effort involved in giving up the status-quo.

5.5 Not Admitting Past Mistakes

It is very human not to admit past mistakes and take responsibility for them, leading to the sunk cost syndrome. It refers to old investments (of usually money, sometimes time), which has become irrecoverable. Such sunk costs should not be part of current (or future) decisions.

If you hired an employee who is not performing up to standards, many people have a hard time admitting the original mistake, and instead invest (via training programs) into the old employee. There are numerous documented cases of former bank managers, who refused to quit supporting old causes and projects, to which they had been committed; despite the fact that outsiders clearly saw that the situation was hopeless. Instead of pulling their support, many bank managers kept investing in the old projects that were no longer viable. It would help to give the old case files to new managers, who do not have the sunk cost syndrome. They would not have any problem discontinuing the old projects which were no longer viable. Hammond, Keeney, and Raiffa in their *Harvard Business Review* article tell an interesting personal story, where one of them consulted a bank during a financial crisis, and found out that this was exactly what was going on.

It is also important in any organization to tolerate mistakes. Do not develop a corporate culture, which immediately punishes for mistakes. We all make mistakes. However, the feature that differentiates good from bad managers is how we deal with mistakes. Whether we learn from mistakes.

5.6 Lives Saved or Lives Lost

Before we can make any decisions or solve a problem, we must first formulate the problem. How we formulate or frame the situation, is of great importance. The framing trap refers to the tendency of people to be influenced by the way a situation or problem is framed (presented). It often works in concert with other traps, such as the status-quo trap or confirming evidence trap.

The first systematic study of framing and its impact was conducted by Tversky and Kahneman (1981). They showed, among other things that it made a difference, whether one framed the problem in terms of lives saved or lives lost (where the total number of lives lost was anyway the same). According to Tversky and Kahneman, people treat gains and losses differently. They react more strongly to negative stimuli than to positive stimuli (of the same size), leading to loss aversion. In particular, certain losses (losses for sure) are frowned upon, and people often want to take their chances with losses (are more risk prone). Treating losses and gains differently may lead to the framing trap.

What can we do about framing? Try out multiple frames. There is not necessarily one and only good way of representing the problem. Be suspicious of the motives of others. They may have a vested interest in presenting the problem in a certain way.

One can also interpret the framing trap in a bit larger context, and discuss what information is provided to decision-makers. Here we refer to the discussion on confirming evidence bias. Many of the same remedies work here too. Governments semi-regularly conduct referendums on important political questions. Finland had a referendum before joining the European Union. The public should be aware that the government controls the information it provides to citizens in connection with referendums. Often the information provided dictates the outcome of the referendum, although in democracies other organizations (besides the government) luckily seek to provide other information pertinent to the choice. It is important to access such information.

5.7 Hubris

Hubris is commonly defined as over-confidence, combined with certain arrogance. Management strategy scholars are increasingly concerned about hubris. They also provide advice how to detect it and how to guard against it. The reader may consult the November 21st, 2016 issue of *Strategy and Leadership:* "The Line Between Confidence and Hubris". The problem is that it may not be easy to detect hubris beforehand. It is easier to detect hubris after the fact. Excessive hubris, which often goes hand in hand with economic boom, can be dangerous, leading to bad decisions and bankruptcies. Typically, hubris implies that the leadership is taking excessive risks, does not pay enough attention to explicit and implicit danger signs, and neglects back-up plans. New ideas and visions are not sufficiently tested. Hubris often works in consortium with the confirming evidence trap, amplifying it.

It is per se natural and good that leaders have visions and bold ideas. Leaders do normally also have confidence. They have received a fine education, and have so far been successful in their business careers. Often, they are hired because of visions and bold ideas. However, one should not be blind to signs of danger. The managers who have narcissistic traits and tend to ignore what others are saying, tend to succumb to hubris.

Whether hubris is more common in some cultures and countries, we are not sure. In the Western world it is certainly common. In the US, before the 2008 financial crisis, hubris was common, in particular among leaders of financial institutions.

What can we do to avoid excessive hubris? It is imperative to question new ideas. The use of a devil's advocate is good. Do not bias your advisers. Moreover, create a corporate culture, where it is encouraged to ask questions and listen to each other.

The prudence trap is the opposite of overconfidence. It implies over-cautiousness. It is not good either, although it has not received as much attention as hubris. The prudence trap fares well in pessimistic, worst-case scenario climate. Managers want to be on the safe side, adjust the margins so that it is extremely unlikely that something goes wrong—adding high costs to the project. Again, healthy cautiousness is good, but not over-cautiousness. You can use the same remedies as we suggested for hubris to counter prudence.

References

Hammond, J., Keeney, R., & Raiffa, H. (1998, September/October). The hidden traps in decision making. *Harvard Business Review*.

Montibeller, G., & Von Winterfeldt, D. (2015). Cognitive and motivational biases in decision and risk analysis. *Risk Analysis, 35*(7), 1230–1251.

Rosenhead, J. (2013). Problem structuring methods. In S. I. Gass & M. C. Fu (Eds.), *Encyclopedia of operations research and management science* (3rd ed., pp. 1162–1172). New York: Springer.

Russo, J. E., & Schoemaker, P. J. H. (1989). *Decision traps: The ten barriers to brilliant decision making and how to overcome them*. New York: Simon & Schuster.

Tversky, A., & Kahneman, D. (1981). The framing of decisions and the psychology of choice. *Science, 211*, 453–458.

Tversky, A., & Simonson, I. (1993). Context dependent preferences. *Management Science, 39*(10), 1179–1189.

Chapter 6
Beware of Decision Traps: The World of Uncertainty

Managers often base their decisions on forecasts; forecasts (or estimates) of future costs, sales, revenue, or the likelihood of future events. For our decision-making, it is critical that such forecasts are as accurate as possible. Humans are notoriously not very good with probabilities. The technical term is that they are not necessarily well-calibrated probability assessors. The only way to improve oneself as a forecaster is to get feedback on, how you did in the past. Your past forecasts and estimates must be on record, so that we can double check how well you did in the past. How accurate have you been? Quite often estimates and forecasts involve probabilities. Besides the decision traps that we have discussed, there are many other traps, which distort our capability to assess (often) subjective probabilities. Some of the most common such traps are:

- Over confidence (poor calibration)
- Memory plays tricks
- Rare is rare

We will define and briefly discuss them. More information can be found in the Tversky and Kahneman's (1974) *Science* article and in the Hammond et al. (1998) *Harvard Business Review* article.

6.1 We Think We Know More Than We Actually Do

People are often overconfident about the accuracy of their forecasts. Overconfidence implies that people think they know more than they actually do. This phenomenon has been documented in many experiments. The first was Alpert and Raiffa (1969).

We illustrate with an example. What is the population of Cairo? This is what the researchers call an almanac-type question, meaning that the correct answer can be found in an almanac (today internet!), however without the almanac or access to the internet, we do not know the correct answer. Hence the population of Cairo is an uncertain quantity to us. Let us try to estimate the (cumulative) probability distribution for it. However, before we do that, it is important that we define the uncertain quantity precisely, in other words are we talking about the population of Cairo proper, or the metro-area. And when? Let us say that Cairo proper and at the end of 2017. (Incidentally, the correct answer is over 12 million, but let us assume that we do not know it.) Estimate values for the five x_i values referring to the 1%, 25%, 50%, 75%, and 99% cumulative probabilities:

P(population of Cairo $< x_1$) = 0.01
P(population of Cairo $< x_2$) = 0.25
P(population of Cairo $< x_3$) = 0.50
P(population of Cairo $< x_4$) = 0.75
P(population of Cairo $< x_5$) = 0.99

Note that the 50% cumulative probability corresponds to your point estimate of the population of Cairo. Let us assume that our answers are: $x_1 = 6$ million, $x_2 = 8$ million, $x_3 = 14$ million, $x_4 = 17$ million, and $x_5 = 20$ million. Now based on one question, we are not able to comment on the quality of our estimates (the calibration). However, if we answer 10 or 100 such (different) questions and each time provide five x-values, we know that in theory the correct answer (to each question) should be below your x_1 in only 1 case (out of 100). Similarly, the correct answer should be below your x_2 values in 25 (out of 100) cases, and so forth. Typically, people's x_1 values are not small enough! Likewise, their x_5 values are not large enough. Hence, people think they know more than they actually know. Their confidence intervals are not wide enough.

The overconfidence bias is a difficult one to correct. Even though the bias has been pointed out to individuals, they are still likely to fall for it. However, practice makes a master.

6.2 Memory Plays Tricks

Recallability trap implies that people overestimate the probability of events, which they can easily think of or recall (from memory). A classic example is an experiment, where people were shown two lists of people having the same number of names on them. Moreover, both lists contained an equal number of men and women. However, in one of the lists, the men were more famous, and in the other list, the women were more famous. Afterwards the subjects were asked to estimate the proportion of women/men in the two lists. Surprise, surprise! Subjects thought that men were more frequent on the list, which contained more famous men, and vice versa. It was simply easier to recall famous people (who we know about), causing the bias.

For the same reason, people typically overestimate the probability of airline accidents, because of the press coverage they receive. They are easy to imagine and recall. Probably most of us remember at least one major airline accident. Yet, percentage-wise they are extremely rare, considering how many daily flights there are in the world. In fact, in 2014 the number of daily flights in the world exceeded 102,000! People do not recall car accidents, they do not even necessarily receive much media coverage. People do remember car accidents, if they or their relatives or friends have been involved in one. The same about accidents caused by driver-less automobiles. When a driver-less Uber car killed a woman, who was walking her bicycle in Tempe, Arizona, there was an uproar. It almost seems that driver-less cars cannot cause any accidents (at least much fewer than cars who have a driver) to be accepted by the general public. (We do realize that the situation is more complex.)

6.3 Rare Is Rare

In the chapter discussing problems with intuition, we discussed an article, which appeared in the *Economist* in early 1990s. We repeat the example.

Example 6.1 Probability of Having a Rare Disease
The probability that a randomly selected person in a population has a certain disease is say 0.001. Let us assume that there is a diagnostic test, which is not perfect. It provides an incorrect diagnosis in 5% of cases. Assume that the test says that we have the disease. This is useful information, despite the fact that the test errs in 5% of the cases. Then what is the probability that we actually have the disease? What do you think? Rather high?

In fact, we can calculate the correct answer using the so-called Bayes formula, which is discussed in introductory statistics courses. The correct answer is about 2%. We think that there are two underlying forces at work, which cause the gross over-estimation of the probability in this case. One is that people are not able to factor in, how common the disease is in the general population (in our case 0.001). Technically we call such probabilities priors. Many may entirely ignore the prior probability. Secondly, the 5% error rate is large, particularly in the medical context (see Appendix).

The analysis becomes more transparent, if we translate the original information from probabilities into frequencies. Because the probability of the disease is 0.001, hence roughly 20 of every 20,000 people have the disease. Of these 20 people, the disease is correctly diagnosed for 19 (95%) people. Moreover, 19,980 (99.9% out of 20,000) people have no disease, but 999 people (5% out of 19,980) are erroneously diagnosed sick. The test gave the result that 1018 ($=19 + 999$) people have the disease, but it plagued actually only 19 people. Thus the chances of diagnosing the disease correctly is only 1.9% ($=19/(19 + 999)*100$)!

6.4 O. J. Simpson Trial

It is not uncommon to calculate the wrong probability correctly, and to use the wrong probability instead of the correct one – to mislead people. A widely known and famous example of this is the murder trial of a former American football player and actor O. J. Simpson of 1994–1995. He was the prime suspect for the murders of his ex-wife Nicole Brown Simpson and her friend, Ronald Goldman on June 13th, 1994. Dershowitz, one of Simpson's defense lawyers, published a book about the case in 1996. A Virginia Tech Statistics Professor published two interesting correspondences in Nature about calculating the probability that Simpson was guilty (Good 1995, 1996). The case is highly interesting and we revisit the probability calculations.

We like to emphasize that there was much evidence presented in the trial, which we did not even seek to access. Hence our example says nothing of Simpson being not guilty or guilty, we merely illustrate interesting facts about the probability calculations.

Example 6.2 O. J. Simpson's Trial Case
In the Simpson trial case, the prosecution and defense fell into the same trap in their argumentation. The prosecution used as evidence that O.J. had battered his ex-wife and argued that exhibited violence "reflects motive to kill". The defense argued against this evidence by claiming that it is very rare that the batterer will murder their spouse. One of the defense attorneys, Alan Dershowitz, clarified this argument in his bestselling book (Dershowitz 1996) by writing that "certainly fewer than 1 out of 2500 men who have a history of beating their domestic partners, go on to murder them". The statement is correct, but misleading. The defense attorney claimed that the probability that a husband or boyfriend who batters their spouse, also murders her is less than 1/2500. (We have no reason to question this figure.)

The purpose of both arguments was to lead the jury to focus on the probability that O.J. murdered his wife, given that he had battered her. Actually, the relevant probability for the jury was different: the probability that a man murders his ex-wife, given that he previously battered her and she was murdered by somebody. This probability turns out to be far from 1/2500. In fact, Good (1996) calculates this probability to be 0.9.

This is a good example that a probability is calculated correctly, but it is the wrong probability. We calculate the correct probability in the Appendix to this chapter.

Some of the relevant facts in the case were as follows. Good (1996) approximated that the probability was 1/20,000 that the victim of a murder was female in the United States in 1994. Good (1996) also estimated that a batterer's probability of murdering their spouse is about 1/2000 per year.

O.J. Simpson was found not guilty.

Appendix: Probability Calculations

Example 6.1 Probability of Having a Rare Disease

Notation:

D: Disease D
$no\ D$: No disease
$P(D) = 0.001$: Probability that a person has D
$P(no\ D) = 0.999$: Probability that a person has not D
T: Positive test result. The accuracy of the test is 5%
$P(T/D) = 0.95$: Probability that test T is positive, if a person has D
$P(T/no\ D) = 0.05$: Probability that test T is positive, if a person has no D
$P(D/T)$: Probability that a person actually has D, when the test says so

We would like to compute the probability $P(D/T)$, which tells us how likely it is that a person has disease D, if the test is positive. Note that this is different from probability $P(T/D)$ to obtain a positive test result for a person with disease D.

Because the accuracy of the test is 5%, to have a correct positive test result for a sick person is 95%. Correspondingly, to have a false positive test result for a healthy person is 5%.

Using Bayes' formula, we may now compute the probability:

$$P(D/T) = \frac{P(T/D)P(D)}{P(T/D)P(D) + P(T/no\ D)P(no\ D)}$$

$$P(D/T) = \frac{0.95 \cdot 0.001}{0.95 \cdot 0.001 + 0.05 \cdot 0.999} = 0.019$$

Hence the probability that a person has the disease, when the test says so, is only about 2%. The reason, why $P(T/D) = 0.95 \gg P(D/T) = 0.02$, is that the test erroneously diagnoses 5% of the healthy persons sick, and the total number of healthy persons is much bigger than that of sick persons.

Example 6.2 O. J. Simpson's Trial Case (Revisited)
We show how to compute the probability that a husband who has a history of beating his wife is also guilty of her murder. Let us first recall what we know[1]:

Event W: Woman was murdered in the US in 1994
$P(W) = 1/20,000$: Prob. that a woman was murdered in the US in 1994

(continued)

---
[1] The numbers are estimated from annual U.S. statistics of year 1994.

Example 6.1 (continued)
Event M: Husband with a history of domestic violence
P(W/M guilty) = 1: Given that the husband M is guilty, the probability that the wife is dead = 1
P(W/not M) = 1/20,000: Prob. that somebody else will kill a woman in 1994
P(M is guilty) = 1/2000: (Prior) prob. that husband M is guilty
P(M is not guilty)
1999/2000: (Prior) prob. that husband M is not guilty
P(M is guilty/W) = ?: The wife is murdered, what is the prob. that the murderer is husband M with a history of domestic violence?

To compute the probability, we use Bayes' formula as before:

$$P(M \text{ is guilty}/W) = \frac{P(W/M \text{ is guilty})P(M \text{ is guilty})}{P(W/M \text{ is guilty})P(M \text{ is guilty}) + P(W/\text{not } M)P(\text{not } M)}$$

$$P(M \text{ is guilty}/W) = \frac{1/2000 \cdot 1}{1/2000 \cdot 1 + 1/20,000 \cdot \left(\frac{1999}{2000}\right)} = 0.91$$

According to Good's calculations, the probability that O.J. Simpson killed his wife is 0.91. This probability obviously ignores all the evidence presented in the trial, and is simply used to demonstrate the probability calculations.

References

Alpert, M., & Raiffa, H. (1969). *A progress report on the training of probability assessors.* Unpublished manuscript. Cambridge, MA: Harvard University.
Dershowitz, A. M. (1996). *Reasonable doubts: The O. J. Simpson case and the criminal justice system.* New York: Simon & Schuster.
Good, I. J. (1995). When batterer turns murderer. *Nature, 375,* 541.
Good, I. J. (1996). When batterer becomes murderer. *Nature, 381,* 481.
Hammond, J., Keeney, R., & Raiffa, H. (1998, September/October). The hidden traps in decision making. *Harvard Business Review.*
Tversky, A., & Kahneman, D. (1974). Judgment under uncertainty: Heuristics and biases. *Science, 185,* 1124–1131.

Chapter 7
The Devil Is in the Details

This chapter discusses in considerable detail many fundamental concepts and features of decision problems, and the complexities of real-world decision-making. Our context is Multiple Criteria Decision Making, where we abstract away from uncertainty. We make the distinction between *Evaluation Problems* and *Design Problems*.

We need to define and discuss the following fundamental concepts in decision-making, particularly in an MCDM context.

- Alternatives
- Criteria
- Goals (targets)
- Objectives
- Attributes (indicators)
- Decision variables
- Value (or utility of the choice)
- Dominance
- Design vs. evaluation problems.

Commonly the dictionary definitions of terms 'criterion', 'goal', and 'objective' are essentially the same. However, in the Multiple Criteria Decision-Making context, it is useful to make a distinction among them (Chankong et al. 1984; Zionts 1989).

7.1 Alternatives

7.1.1 Known Alternatives and Decision Variables

Decision alternatives can be listed (enumerated) or they can be designed with the help of mathematical restrictions (inequalities, constraints).

If all relevant decision alternatives are known, the decision problem becomes simpler. An example of such a case is the choice of a restaurant in downtown Helsinki. Let us assume that we have already decided to eat Thai food. All the Thai food restaurants in downtown Helsinki can quickly be listed. We are not saying that the choice among the Thai restaurants is necessarily simple. What we are saying is that knowing all the available alternatives makes the choice simpler.

As an example of the latter (design) situation, we may consider the production planning problem with an aim to maximize profits by selling products. What we can produce (and sell) is restricted by available machine capacity, raw materials, and financial resources. These resource constraints (implicitly) characterize the alternatives. Even if we cannot name a specific alternative or list them, we know the set from which the alternatives are chosen. In this case, the alternatives are defined indirectly (implicitly). The amounts of different products define the alternatives.

For example, the most preferred alternative might be 'zero units of product 1, five units of product 2, six units of product 3', etc. In technical lingo (in a design situation), the different production amounts, which are used to define alternatives, are called decision variables. Naturally, decision variables are by no means limited to production amounts of different products. They are quantities (described by mathematical symbols) that represent levels of activity of an organization.

7.1.2 Alternatives Emerging Over Time

A classic example of the case, where all alternatives are initially not known, is the choice of a spouse, also known as the secretary problem. We would like to choose the 'best' possible spouse (however we define that), but we do not know how many (and how good) spouse candidates we will meet and when. At some point, if we would like to get married, we have to stop searching and choose a partner. A complicating feature of the problem is, however, that if we at some point reject a spouse candidate, we (normally) are not able to reconsider her/him, because (s)he has moved on with her/his life.

This problem has been studied extensively in the fields of applied probability, statistics, and decision theory. For this problem there exists a simple mathematical solution, provided that we know or are able to estimate the number of potential candidates we will meet during our life time. The optimal stopping rule (which we do not prove here; for a proof see Raiffa et al. 2007, p. 163) tells us to always reject the first n/e candidates (who are 'tested') and then to choose the one who is better than any of the previously considered ones (n is the total number of candidates and e is the so-called Neper number, base of the natural logarithm ($=2.718$)). For instance, if we think that we will meet ten candidates (during our lifetime), then the optimal strategy is to let first three go by ($10/2.718 = 3.7$) and accept the first one, who is better than any of the previously considered ones. The probability to find the best spousal candidate is about 0.4 ($\approx 1/2.718$), which may not be ideal, but is the best we can

7.1 Alternatives

(mathematically) do. Note that in this problem we can set up a decision rule in advance and use it.

A more realistic variation of the secretary problem is more demanding. Let us assume that we are going to hire a secretary for our firm. First, we specify which kind of requirements we expect of the candidates and publish or post a call for applicants in a newspaper or on the web. A group of applicants will likely respond to our ad. Now we have to make two decisions: 1) to find the best candidate from the group of current applicants, and 2) to decide whether we try to find better candidates with a new call. In the first decision, we presumably evaluate the candidates with several criteria and find the one who meets our criteria best. In the second decision, we have to strike a balance between finding a better candidate (and how much better) and the cost of continuing the search.

In both problems, several of the alternatives are initially not known, but the problems are different. In the first one, the choice is straightforward provided that we follow our decision rule. The second problem requires more advanced techniques to solve.

7.1.3 Not Realizing Viable Alternatives

It is also possible that we do not recognize all (available) alternatives. For example, if we would like to go as quickly as possible (assume only one criterion) from place A to place B, it is possible that we only think of renting a car or using a bus. Perhaps we do not even think of the possibility to take a taxi or ask a friend or relative to give us a ride, assuming that we do not ourselves have access to a car.

Let us consider another simple example, which demonstrates how confined our mind sometimes is to figure out possible solutions to problems:

> **Example 7.1 Car Accident**
> A man and his son ended up in a car accident, where the father died and the seriously injured son was taken to the hospital. Because the son had a bad head injury, a brain surgeon (self-confident and arrogant according to colleagues) was called to see the boy. "He is my son!", the doctor cried in horror. How is this possible? (The solution is provided in Appendix).

7.1.4 Too Many Alternatives

There exist decision situations, in which we have good reasons to eliminate alternatives. This may happen, if the number of alternatives is too large to consider (without any support system). A typical approach to the problem (and to limit the number of alternatives) is to eliminate some alternatives by using simple upper/lower limits to

Table 7.1 A subset of flats for sale

Flats	Price (€)	# of Bedrooms	Location
MM	300,000	3	Espoo
NN	400,000	2	Helsinki

the criteria (as described in Chap. 4). This may, however, lead to rejecting the alternative which might turn out to be the most preferred one. The situation is illustrated in Table 7.1.

Assume that alternatives 'MM' and 'NN' are two flats in a large data set, and the DM decides to make a quick initial search using only three criteria 'Price', '# of Bedrooms', and 'Location'. Because the DM prefers Helsinki to Espoo, she may think that the differences in the other two criterion values are not big enough to change her preference in favor of Espoo, and she rejects alternative MM. What if the flats are located in the same neighborhood and the border of the two cities runs between the houses. In this case, the preference of the DM might be different. However, this solution was eliminated from further consideration in our initial search.

7.2 Criteria

7.2.1 One vs. Multiple Criteria

Sometimes it is possible to judge decision alternatives just using one criterion, such as profit or cost. Depending on how the problem is defined, optimizing such a criterion is a pure math problem; no human interaction is needed. In our book we consider the more interesting case, which involves multiple criteria. Keeney and Raiffa (1976) in their classic book on multiple objective decision making, discuss the problem of choosing the location of an airport for Mexico City in the 1970s. The problem was highly complex and very political. One could easily list the following criteria[1]:

- (Minimize) the costs to the federal government.
- (Raise) the capacity of airport facilities.
- (Improve) the safety of the system.
- (Reduce) noise levels.
- (Reduce) access time to users.
- (Minimize) displacement of people for expansion.
- (Improve) regional development (roads).
- (Achieve) political aims.

---

[1]Note that the criteria, except the last one, are defined as objectives, if we remove the parentheses (but not the words in the parentheses). The last one is a goal.

In the corporate world, it is often said that the 'bottom line' (that is profit) is the only thing that matters. Obviously, profits are important for a business company, because otherwise it could not function. However, it is very important what risks the company takes to achieve certain profits. Moreover, companies should discuss the short term versus long term, in other words, they need to decide (when discussing profits), what is the time frame. In addition to profits, companies usually care about the well-being of its employees (perhaps the leadership thinks that happier employees are more productive ...). Nowadays, there is also considerable emphasis on 'green values' or 'sustainable development'. Obviously, employee well-being and sustainable development need to be defined.

Seldom can we find a so-called dominating alternative, which would be best in terms of all criteria: the cheapest and best product, with longest warranty, delivered immediately. If the world were this simple, our choice problem would be easy. We would naturally choose this alternative, which dominates all other alternatives. Normally, however, the criteria are conflicting. The cheapest product is not the best and does not have the longest warranty. Those of us who have invested in the stock market, have quickly learned that we cannot at the same time maximize returns and minimize risks. In such cases, the decision-maker must make value tradeoffs. In other words, the decision-maker is faced with the problem of trading-off the achievement in one criterion against another.

7.2.2 Criteria vs. Goals and Objectives

Criterion is the basis for evaluating decision alternatives. It is a measure of performance used to evaluate decision alternatives. It may be quantitative or qualitative, although we commonly express originally qualitative criteria with some numeric scale. Examples are profits, costs, quality, pleasure, efficiency, profitability, etc. When we would like to express 'how', we use the terms goals, targets, or objectives.

Goal (Synonymous with Target) refers to a state we would like to achieve. It is something either achieved or not. For example, 'our market share next year should be 30%' is a goal. Often a goal is something concrete such as in the example, but we also talk about 'soft' goals: 'next year our family would like to travel to Greece for holidays'.

Objective is something to be pursued to its fullest. For example, a manager may want to say that next year we have to 'improve our cost efficiency' or 'raise market share'—as much as possible.

7.2.3 Attributes and Indicators

Attributes and indicators are used to characterize the alternatives. For instance, when we are in the process of hiring a secretary, we collect pieces of information about the applicants: education, work experience, IT-related skills, references from previous jobs, fit to the job, etc. The attributes provide a basis for the criteria. In the example, the criteria might be potential performance, ambition, self-confidence, etc. Of course, such criteria are not easily defined and measured. The attributes are not usually the same as criteria, but they may be used to describe criteria.

There is a slight difference between indicators and attributes. An attribute refers to general features used as the basis for defining the decision-relevant criteria. If an attribute has a numeric representation or some other specific format, we sometimes call it an indicator. It is fashionable to talk about companies' Key Performance Indicators (KPIs), which measure how effectively a company is achieving key business objectives. The KPIs are always measurable.

In our secretary recruiting example, we mentioned 'experience' as one of the attributes. Some features of this attribute can be presented via indicators, such as 'the length of work experience'. However, 'what type of experience' a person has, is better described in a 'soft' way.

The number of attributes may be quite large and the information pertaining to them not necessarily very systematically collected. Instead, for good decision-making, the number of criteria cannot be very high or the criteria have to be classified. The classification can be made by constructing a hierarchical tree. The building of a criterion hierarchy is an advisable and standard approach used in the famous Analytic Hierarchy Process (AHP) (Saaty 1982, also see Hämäläinen and Seppäläinen 1986). The AHP is a structured technique for organizing and analyzing complex decisions.

7.2.4 Qualitative vs. Quantitative Criteria

A criterion may be quantitative (presented numerically), or it may be qualitative. Most of our examples in our book concern quantitative criteria. Sometimes (in fact frequently) qualitative criteria are expressed with a numerical scale (for example a Likert scale: 1, 2, 3 ... 7) (7 best). As an example of purely qualitative criteria, we use the evaluation of dogs in a dog show. We will see from the example that judges use (qualitative) criteria, although their approach is typically holistic.

> **Example 7.2 Evaluation of Show Dogs**
> "Judges use established standards for an ideal dog, although they may vary. In addition to the physical ideal, the standard specifies how the dog should move, or "gait", and what its temperament should be. Male and female dogs are

(continued)

Example 7.2 (continued)
judged separately. When the judge evaluates your dog, s(he) compares her/him to the established ideal, judging height, weight, coat quality and coloring, overall build and appearance. She looks at specific physical traits, watches the dog's movement, and observes demeanor and behavior." The judge has the freedom to use the underlying criteria (s)he wants in evaluating the dogs. Finally, (s)he ranks the dogs using his/her overall impression without even trying to systematically aggregate the criteria. (Dog Show Requirements by Jane Meggitt: https://pets.thenest.com/dog-show-requirements-11723.html).

7.2.5 Structure of Criteria and Their Possible Dependence

Sometimes the criteria have a natural hierarchical structure. In this case the evaluations made at the lower level(s) have to be aggregated to the upper level(s), where the final choice is made. Typically, the performance of a company depends on the performance of its different divisions. The management has to gather information from the lower level and to make the overall evaluation at the top level. We will discuss at some length the aggregation of criteria in connection with the Analytic Hierarchy Process.

Normally criteria are to some extent dependent (correlated). And that is alright. However, we must be aware of the case of extreme dependence. In such cases, we have to take the dependence into account. For instance, when family members are gathered together to choose a place for spending holidays, they may decide to use criteria, such as price and suitability of the location for hiking, fishing, hunting, swimming, golfing, etc. It may happen that certain alternatives are good (or poor) in terms of all (or most) "hobby criteria". Hence "hobby criteria" dominate the choice (simply because there are so many of them), even if the purpose is to "balance" the price and recreational activities.

7.2.6 Known vs. Unknown Criteria

Our book is about decision-making in the presence of multiple criteria. Our argument is that criteria matter (generally). What those criteria are, is sometimes clear, but sometimes it requires thought to decide about the decision-relevant criteria. We do, however, realize that in many (simple?) every-day problems people do not even think about criteria. Think about buying a new hat! You just buy a hat which pleases you. No matter, what the criteria are. You do not even try to think, why the hat you bought, pleases you.

There are many decision problems, in which all criteria are not known or are not used in decision-making, because

- You do not recognize all decision-relevant criteria, or
- You simplify the problem by ignoring some (less important?) criteria, or
- You are not willing to explicitly state your criteria.

It is not uncommon that we simplify the problem, because its structure is too complicated and humans are unable to focus attention to very many criteria simultaneously. The classic paper by Miller from 1956 suggests that one should not use more than some seven criteria in decision-making.

Assume, for instance, that you are choosing a hotel where to spend your beach holidays. Usually, you may check in advance how far the hotel is from the beach, how much you have to pay for the flight and hotel, how many stars the hotel has, and is breakfast included or not. It is possible that these are your most important criteria, but many people are also interested in knowing how crowded the beach is, is it easy to rent beach chairs, how difficult it is to call a taxi to pick you up from the beach, etc. Researching about all these factors takes time and effort.

In case you have to discuss or defend your decision in front of your peers or employees or even publicly, it is not uncommon that many people do not reveal all of their criteria. For instance, assume you are hiring a new employee and one of the applicants is a foreigner. If you are reluctant to hire a foreigner, it is unlikely that you openly make the statement that you do not want to hire him/her (unless it is clear that the job requires fluency in Finnish language). Instead, you try to use other criteria to argue why we should hire somebody else. The more criteria you use, the easier it is for you to defend your choice. An excellent example of the existence of hidden (not outspoken) criteria was a debate that took place in the Finnish Parliament on October 16, 2018. The entire discussion was broadcast on live TV.

> **Example 7.3 A Debate in the Finnish Parliament**
> The Government of Finland is about to propose new legislation, which would make it easier for small companies (at most ten employees) to lay-off people. The government argues that their proposal is an efficient way to improve employment. Strong arguments against the legislation have been presented by the left-wing parties in the Parliament and labor unions. Before officially proposing this new legislation, the Government (Cabinet) organized a general discussion about it in the Parliament. The discussion was highly interesting.
>
> It was especially important to the Members of the Parliament (MPs) to be visible during the debate, because the Parliament elections were held in April 2019 in Finland. The MPs wanted to eagerly discuss and present the arguments they believed to be important for their voters. The MPs of the left-wing parties mainly spoke about inequality and firing of employees to boost corporate profits. An MP even argued that the proposed legislation will make it more difficult to employ people in small companies. The right-wing MPs had contrary arguments and they emphasized positive effects for the employment. The threshold to hire new people becomes much lower. They were very
>
> (continued)

Example 7.3 (continued)
careful not to underscore that the proposed legislation would increase the freedom of the employers to lay-off people.

Interestingly, none of the MPs explicitly stated that their most important (hidden) criterion was to present arguments, which appealed to their potential voters.

It is important that your criteria are something that you think are important and relevant for your decision. You must think hard, whether you have left out an important criterion. They should also be something that can be operationalized, that is measured. Generally, it is a good idea to keep the number of criteria relatively small, focusing on the important ones. The criteria should also measure (relatively speaking) different aspects of the problem, although there is usually some form of dependence between them.

You must also decide, whether a criterion is of the 'maximizing' type (profits) or 'minimizing' type (costs), or perhaps you want to achieve a target value for a criterion, such as a target profit. In this case, you typically want to minimize the deviations from the target.

The decision-relevant criteria should be such that (from the boss's perspective) the sub-bosses (representing divisions, units) cannot artificially manipulate them. We cite an example from the academia. When measuring the research output of different schools or departments in a university, it might on surface be a good idea to use as one of the criteria 'number of times professors' articles have been downloaded'. The number of downloads reflects how popular the article is and is a surrogate measure for its impact. (This information is available from the publishers.) However, when people and departments know that they are being judged based on how many times their articles have been downloaded, they may themselves spend days downloading their papers, or ask their graduate students to do this, or device a robot to download their articles! When this happens, obviously, number of downloads no longer is a relevant decision criterion.

7.2.7 Certainty vs. Uncertainty in the Criterion Values

If we can specify without uncertainty, how well each alternative fulfills the specified criteria, we talk about a decision problem under certainty. In many consumer choice problems, each available alternative can be specified with criterion values assumed to be known with certainty. (Of course, there could be uncertainty, how long the product lasts.) Let us assume that we want to buy lumber for our house construction project. To simplify matters, let us further assume that we have decided what type of lumber we want. Then the choice problem has two criteria: cost and time of delivery. If the cheapest lumber yard offers fastest delivery, the problem is simple. This is, however, not always the case. Often there is a tradeoff between price and delivery terms. Those lumber yards which deliver faster are often more expensive. Then we as consumers must think hard whether the faster delivery is worth the extra cost.

There are many decision problems which involve uncertainty in the criterion values. A classic example is oil-drilling.

> **Example 7.4 Oil Drilling**
> Moskowitz and Wright (1975) describe a simple problem where the oil wildcatter has only two options: to drill or not to drill in a specific site. The uncertainty originates from the fact, whether the hole is dry, wet or soaking with oil. The cost of drilling is 700,000 dollars. If the well is judged to be soaking, the revenue is estimated to be 2.7 million dollars. If the well is wet, the revenue is 1.2 million dollars. If we do not drill, no gain, no pain.

In this problem, there is only one criterion 'revenue' and two alternatives 'to drill' or 'not to drill'. The problem is difficult, because we do not know the value of the revenue in case we decide to drill. If we do not drill, we lose nothing, but nothing is gained either. If we can reliably model uncertainty via probabilities, the problem simplifies. The question, however, is how comfortable are humans making reliable probability assessments. There is lots of literature on the subject, some critical.

In this case, we assume that the decision whether we should drill or not, depends on the likelihood (or probability) that the well is soaking or wet or dry. If we judge it to be highly likely that the well is soaking, we should probably go ahead, in particular if the company is big enough that they would survive the cost of drilling (and no oil). Many decision scientists estimate probabilities for what they call 'states of nature' (the well is dry, wet, or soaking). In the Moskowitz-Wright textbook, they specify the following probabilities for the three 'states of nature':

$$P(\text{dry}) = 0.5, P(\text{wet}) = 0.3, \text{ and } P(\text{soaking}) = 0.2.$$

Notation '$P(\text{dry}) = 0.5$' means 'the probability is 0.5 that the well is dry'.

Then the authors suggest that we calculate the expected value (EV) (=the weighted mean) of both alternatives (drill, not drill) by multiplying the outcomes with the probabilities. Hence:

$$EV(\text{not drill}) = 0 * 0.5 + 0 * 0.3 + 0 * 0.2 = 0$$

$$EV(\text{drill}) = -700,000 * 0.5 + 1.2 \text{ million} * 0.3 + 2.7 \text{ million} * 0.2$$
$$= 550,000 \text{ dollars}$$

Since the expected value of the drill option is higher, we suggest to drill. However, the problem is not quite this simple. The probabilities of the different states are highly uncertain. It is not uncommon that in such a situation, the wildcatter would want to obtain seismic information, to improve the probability estimates.

7.3 Dominance

Note, however, that the seismic information is usually not perfect (but highly imperfect). Another complicating factor in the oil drilling problem is the decision-maker's risk attitude, in other words whether she or he is risk neutral, risk averse or risk prone. In the above simple example, we have assumed that the decision-maker is risk neutral, allowing us to work with expected (monetary) values. We illustrate the concepts 'risk neutral', 'risk averse', and 'risk prone' with the following situation.

Assume that somebody is interested in buying the rights to drill. If the wildcatter asks for 550,000 dollars (same as expected value of drilling) for the rights and the buyer is indifferent between to buy or not to buy, then (s)he is risk neutral. If (s)he is willing to buy the rights for a higher price, then (s)he is risk prone. Correspondingly, (s)he is risk averse, if (s)he buys the rights only if the price is lower than the expected value 550,000.

We realize that we do not always know for certain the criterion values and understand the need for dealing with the uncertainty of criterion values. There is an alternative, avoiding formally introducing probabilities into decision-making, namely scenario analysis. In our book, we discuss this technique. For example, in the example where we are investing the mother-in-law's money, we never introduced probabilities for different states of the economy. Instead, we regarded the different states as different scenarios (criteria).

7.3 Dominance

If we have only one criterion to be maximized or minimized, it is easy to rank alternatives based on the values of that criterion. The rank order in case of a single criterion is not debatable. The alternative with the maximal criterion value is clearly best or the most preferred one. In Table 7.2, we have listed three (hypothetical and similar) firms A, B, and C whose performance is evaluated with three criteria 'market share', 'profits', and 'total costs'. If we would like to rank them using only one criterion 'profits', it is simple to do: B is best, A the second best, and C the worst. If we use 'total costs', the rank order is the same. Instead, 'market share' gives a quite different rank order: A, C, and B.

In Multiple Criteria Decision Making (MCDM), it is not possible to find the best rank order or alternative without interacting with the decision-maker. Assume that the performance of firms A and B is evaluated with two criteria 'market share' and 'profits'. The market share of A is better than B's. Instead B is better than A in terms of 'profits'.

Table 7.2 Comparing firms

Firms	Market share (%)	Profits €	Costs €
A	10	8,000,000	15,000,000
B	5	13,000,000	14,000,000
C	8	7,000,000	18,000,000

When a decision-maker is asked to evaluate alternatives A and B on both criteria, the rank order depends on her preferences. There is no objective way to rank the firms—without additional information. If the decision-maker thinks that profits is more important than market share, she may prefer B to A. We cannot be sure, whether this choice is wise or not. Of course, somebody may criticize the decision-maker's preferences, but this is a different issue. Both firms are so called non-dominated alternatives. If we add a third criterion 'total costs', the dominance structure in our example does not change. Even if B has better values in terms of profits and costs, the market share of C is better. Their mutual rank order still depends on the decision-maker's preferences.

Assume that we add a third alternative C for the considerations. If we compare B and C, there is no objective way to rank them. The profits and costs of B are better than C's, but the market share of C is better. Thus, we need a decision-maker to say which one is preferred. However, the situation is different if we compare A and C. All criterion values of firm C are worse than that of A. In this case, we say that C is dominated by A. Thus, A is objectively better than C. In case B is preferred to A, we may conclude that B is preferred to C as well. Because C is worse than A on all criteria, we do not need a decision-maker to rank B and C.

The dominance structure plays an important role in Multiple Criteria Decision Making. If we try to find the most preferred alternative, only the non-dominated alternatives are interesting. However, if our purpose is to rank alternatives or to select the most preferred set, the situation changes. Then all chosen alternatives are not necessarily non-dominated, but at least one is. If in our example the DM is asked to choose two best alternatives, the reasonable choice is A and C. In this case, she considers market share very important. A reasonable choice is also A and B, because both are non-dominated. Instead, the choice of B and C is not wise.

How to find the best (most preferred) solution is one of the key problems in the field of MCDM. To accomplish this, in addition to Mathematics and Computer Science, knowledge of behavioral science is needed.

7.4 Value (or Utility)

'Value' of an alternative to a decision-maker is its desirability or worth. It is inherently subjective, and value comparisons across individuals are difficult. However, individuals can reasonably be expected to tell us, which alternative (out of two or a small set) they value highest. 'Value' is a theoretical concept, and we do not seek to explicitly measure how valuable different alternatives are. Rather our goal is to help decision-makers find their Most Preferred Alternative. Some scholars use interchangeably 'value' and 'utility', but we prefer to use the term 'value' in the (riskless) MCDM context.

7.5 Number of Decision-Makers

When using the term 'decision-maker', most people probably think of one person who makes decisions. Often this is true, but not always. Sometimes, and this is often the case in the public sector, it is a group or committee who makes the decisions. The decision-making may be based on reaching a consensus or the use of some voting scheme, such as simple majority. It is also not uncommon that one in the group (for example the CEO) has full decision-making power and the others in the group are advisors. The final decision is made by the person who is responsible for the consequences of the decision. One possibility is that decision-making is distributed in an organization. Many people at different levels of an organization make decisions and some final alternative proposals are composed for the CEO, who will choose the best one from the proposals—or reject them all.

Decision-making may also be viewed as a process, instead of happening at a specific point in time. The whole organization acts towards a final goal, but different levels have their own sub-goals, which contribute to the final overall goal.

If the problem situation involves more than one decision-maker, it is generally referred to as a negotiation (or a group decision-making situation). The study of negotiations is an exciting and rich field, where practitioners can learn from theory and vice versa. We refer to Raiffa's excellent book on negotiation analysis (2007). The book covers win-lose negotiations, although the emphasis is on win-win negotiations. There are also many excellent popular negotiation texts, such as Fisher et al. (2011). Our book has a short chapter on negotiations.

7.6 Design Problems

An evaluation problem is one where we explicitly can list all decision alternatives. A design problem is one where we implicitly define alternatives with the help of mathematical restrictions (called constraints). We have at length discussed evaluation problems, and they are the primary focus of our book. However, for completeness sake, we want to introduce the rudiments of a design problem.

With the help of the following production planning problem we illustrate the design problem. The problem has only one criterion.

Table 7.3 Data for production planning problem

	Product 1	Product 2	Product 3		Availability
Machine hours	1.5	1.0	1.6	$\leq$	9
Man hours	1.0	2.0	1.0	$\leq$	10
Critical material 1	9.0	19.5	7.5	$\leq$	96
Critical material 2	7.0	20.0	9.0	$\leq$	96
Profits	4	5	3	$\rightarrow$	Max

Table 7.4 Experimental calculations with different product amounts

Product combos	Mach. H.	Man H.	Cr. Mat. 1	Cr. Mat. 2	Profits
A (1,1,5)	10.5	8	66	72	24
B (1,1,1)	6.1	8	75	76	22
C (1,2,3)	8.3	8	70.5	74	23
D (3,3,1)	9.1	10	93	90	30
E (2,3,2)	9.2	10	91.5	92	29
F (3,3,0)	7.5	9	85.5	81	27

Example 7.5 Production Planning
The problem for a company is to decide, how much of three products to produce to maximize profits. For simplicity, we assume that all produced products can be sold. Hence the more we produce (and sell) of the three products, the larger our profits. The production is, however, limited by the available machine-hours and man-hours (personnel). Furthermore, the production of the three products requires the use of so called critical materials, which are also in limited supply. Table 7.3 below tells the availability of all the resources, also how much a one-unit production of each product consumes each resource. The last row tells the unit profits from producing and selling each product.

Let us assume that the decision-maker tries to solve the problem without any support. (S)he has conducted six experiments (on paper) A-F with different amounts of products 1, 2, and 3. The required resources and generated profits are given as columns in the following Table 7.4. For instance, alternative A is generated by setting value one to products 1 and 2, and 5 to product 3. Note that A somewhat exceeds available machine hours (limit 9). Whether this is possible or not, we do not know. To choose the most preferred solution from among these six alternatives is an evaluation problem. Alternatives do now 'exist' and they are generated by means of decision variables: production amounts of products 1, 2, and 3. Obviously, the best alternative to the decision-maker is D, even if the original requirement of available machine hours is a bit exceeded.

However, D is not necessarily the best combination, which can be achieved. The optimal solution is found by using Linear Programming, a single-objective optimization method. The main principle is quite easy to understand. We do not fix the values of the decision variables in advance, but let the system find optimal values for them. We have to define the formulae for requirements. For instance, the formula for available machine-hours is written as

$$1.5x_1 + x_2 + 1.6x_3 \leq 9,$$

7.7 Why Are Some Choices Difficult?

Table 7.5 The optimal solution of the production planning problem

Prods.	Mach. H.	Man H.	Cr. Mat. 1	Cr. Mat. 2	Profits
G(4,3,0)	9	10	94.5	88	31

where x_1, x_2, and x_3 refer to the undefined (presently unknown) values of product 1, 2, and 3.

In the same way, we write the equations for the other restrictions or constraints. Furthermore, we have to specify that we would like to optimize (maximize) profits, that is:

$$4x_1 + 5x_2 + 3x_3 \rightarrow \max,$$

where the coefficients are the unit profits from the three products.

When the alternatives are defined by using weighted sums of (the values of) decision variables and constraints which specify the possible alternatives, we have a design problem. Possible alternatives are called feasible solutions.

To solve a Linear Programming problem, you do not have to know how to do it, but you have to be able to give the required information for the Linear Programming software. The problem can be solved with Excel Solver. Solver is a Microsoft Excel add-in program you can use to find an optimal (maximum or minimum) value for a formula in one cell—called the objective cell—subject to constraints, or limits, on the values of other formula cells on a worksheet. In the internet you can find tutorials for using Excel Solver. Excellent textbooks are Balakrishnan et al. (2013) and Moore and Weatherford (2001).

The 'changing cells' (the decision variables) would be the production amounts of each product, to be optimally determined by Excel Solver. Each of the rows represents a resource constraint.

The optimal solution of the production planning problem solved by using Excel Solver is produced in (Table 7.5):

In an Appendix to this chapter, we present the mathematical formulation for the problem. In Chap. 12 (Subsection 12.4) we return to this problem and show how it can be solved by using Multiple Objective Linear Programming (MOLP).

7.7 Why Are Some Choices Difficult?

There are many reasons why a choice problem may be difficult. One obvious reason may be uncertainty regarding the outcomes. But even if we abstract from uncertainty, there may be various reasons why the choice is difficult. There may be very many good alternatives, and it is hard to decide on the "best", since complex tradeoffs are involved. Sometimes there are very many criteria.

However, sometimes there are just two alternatives (and a reasonable number of criteria), from which we must choose. The choice is difficult, if we do not like either alternative—or if we like both alternatives. The former case reminds us of a presidential election in Finland during the 1990s. At the second round the choice was between a social democratic male and a conservative female representing the Swedish Party. We can understand the difficulty of some of our conservative male friends of voting for either candidate. They would not want to vote for a social democrat, nor a Swedish speaking woman!

Often it may happen that a DM will change her mind during the evaluation process (due to learning, or simply out of curiosity), and may even want to reconsider some of the alternatives previously discarded.

7.8 What are Better Decisions in an MCDM Context?

Why do we need the concept of 'dominance'? If our problem only had one criterion (to be optimized), we would have no need for this concept. Instead, we could mathematically solve for the best solution. The situation is different when we have multiple criteria. Usually, optimizing each criterion separately leads to different solutions (or alternatives). Which alternative the DM finally chooses, depends on how she values each of the criteria. The final (chosen) alternative depends on the decision-maker's preferences. We may not know her preferences very well (apriori), but at least we know that it is unwise to choose a dominated alternative.

What is a 'wise' decision, is somewhat a complex question. In our book we simplify and state that a wise decision is a nondominated alternative in an MCDM context. We may also call non-dominated alternatives rational, because it would be irrational to choose a dominated alternative.

For the dominance concept to work properly, we assume that we have correctly identified all criteria (including their numerical values), and that there are no hidden criteria. We also assume that we have been able to list all relevant decision alternatives. Under such (sometimes perhaps unrealistic) assumptions, it would not be wise for a person to choose a dominated alternative, because she can do better in terms of some criteria, and not worse in any criteria. In a recruiting context, why would you want to recruit a candidate who is less experienced, less intelligent, and wants a higher pay than another person? Perhaps the smartest and most experienced person is not a team-player? In that case, it would be better to have 'team player' (somehow rated) as an explicit criterion, and the smartest and most experienced person would no longer dominate the other candidates.

Appendix: Car Accident and Production Planning

Car Accident

The brain doctor is a woman. She is the mother of the son. The problem is made tricky by attaching some supposedly 'male' adjectives to the doctor: arrogant and self-confident.

Production Planning

A single-objective Linear Programming formulation for the production planning problem:

$$\begin{aligned}
\text{maximize} \quad & 4x_1 + 5x_2 + 3x_3 \\
& 1.5x_1 + x_2 + 1.6x_3 \leq 9 \\
& x_1 + 2x_2 + x_3 \leq 10 \\
& 9x_1 + 19.5x_2 + 7.5x_3 \leq 96 \\
& 7x_1 + 20x_2 + 9x_3 \leq 96 \\
& x_1, x_2, x_3 \geq 0
\end{aligned}$$

References

Balakrishnan, N., Render, B., & Stair, R. (2013). *Managerial decision modeling with spreadsheets* (3rd ed.). Upper Saddle River, NJ: Pearson.

Chankong, V., Haimes, Y. Y., Thadathil, J., & Zionts, S. (1984). Multiple criteria optimization: A state of the art review. In Y. Y. Haimes & V. Chankong (Eds.), *Decision making with multiple objectives* (pp. 36–90). Heidelberg: Springer.

Fisher, R., Ury, W., & Patton, B. (2011). *Getting to yes: Negotiating agreement without giving in*. New York: Penquin Books.

Hämäläinen, R. P., & Seppäläinen, T. O. (1986). The analytic network process in energy policy planning. *Socio-Economic Planning Sciences, 20*(6), 399–405.

Keeney, R., & Raiffa, H. (1976). *Decisions with multiple objectives: Preferences and value tradeoffs*. New York: Wiley.

Miller, G. (1956). The magical number seven, plus or minus two: Some limits on our capacity for processing information. *Psychological Review, 101*(2), 343–352.

Moore, J. H., & Weatherford, L. R. (2001). *Decision modeling with Microsoft Excel* (6th ed.). Upper Saddle River, NJ: Prentice Hall.

Moskowitz, H., & Wright, G. (1975). *Management science: An experiential approach*. Iowa: Kendall/Hunt.

Raiffa, H., Richardson, J., & Metcalfe, D. (2007). *Negotiation analysis*. Cambridge, MA: The Belknap Press.

Saaty, T. L. (1982). *Decision making for leaders: The analytic hierarchy process for decisions in a complex world*. Pittsburgh, PA: RWS Publications.

Zionts, S. (1989). Multiple criteria mathematical programming. In B. Karpak & S. Zionts (Eds.), *Multiple criteria decision making and risk analysis using microcomputers* (NATO ASI Series F) (Vol. 56, pp. 7–60). Berlin: Springer.

Chapter 8
A Picture Is Worth a Thousand Words

According to a Chinese proverb, "a picture is worth a thousand words". This is also very true, when describing and comparing multiple criteria decision alternatives, in particular, when there are many criteria and many alternatives. It is much easier for the decision-maker to have a holistic view of the situation, if instead of (or in addition to) numeric information, suitable visualization techniques are used.

We next discuss various visualization techniques originating from statistics, which have proven useful in the Multiple Criteria Decision Making framework. We focus on fundamental visualization techniques. From the perspective of visualization, the complexity depends on the number of criteria and the number of alternatives. A problem may be complex due to having a large number of alternatives and a small number of criteria, or the other way around, although the nature of the complexity is different. Different visualization techniques are required for each case. Good visuals help the DM to obtain a holistic perception of the available alternatives.

In descriptive statistics, computer graphics is widely used to illustrate numerical information by producing standard visual representations (bar charts, line graphs, pie charts, etc.). More advanced visualization techniques, for example, Andrews curves (Andrews 1972) and Chernoff faces (Chernoff 1973) have also been proposed. These techniques have been developed for problems, in which the main purpose is to obtain a holistic view of the data and/or to identify clusters, outliers, etc. In the multiple criteria framework, an additional requirement is to provide the DM with information (value information) for articulating preferences.

We review basic and more advanced visualization techniques, which are useful for illustrating a single alternative or a set of alternatives.

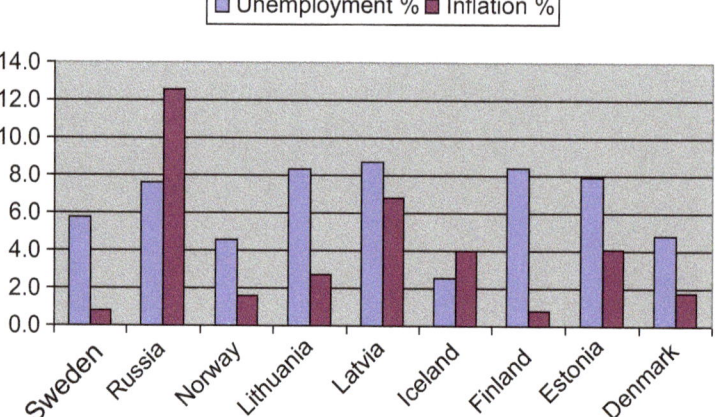

Fig. 8.1 Illustrating unemployment and inflation rates with a bar chart

8.1 Visual Representation of Numerical Data

Graphical techniques have been considered extremely useful by statisticians in analyzing and illustrating data. However, they have not been utilized by the MCDM- community to their full potential. Standard graphical techniques, such as bar charts, value paths, line graphs, etc., have a common feature: they provide an alternative representation for numerical data and numerical values can be "read" (sometimes roughly) from the visual representation as well. More information can be found in any statistics book, for example Levine et al. (2006).

8.1.1 Bar Charts, Line Graphs, and Scatter Plots

Next, we discuss bar charts, line graphs, and scatter plots. As an example, we use a small data set illustrating the unemployment rate (%) and inflation rate (%) in nine countries.

The bar charts are a standard technique to summarize frequency data, and they are called histograms in this context.[1] In Fig. 8.1, we use a bar chart to represent the (values of) unemployment rate (%) and inflation rate (%) of each of the nine countries. This is customary in a multiple criteria framework, where instead of summary data the criterion values of various alternatives (in our example, countries) are more interesting. At one glance we obtain useful information about the values of our "criteria" (unemployment rate (%) and inflation rate (%)) describing the health of the economy in different countries.

---

[1] The graph is based on preliminary data from year 2005.

8.1 Visual Representation of Numerical Data

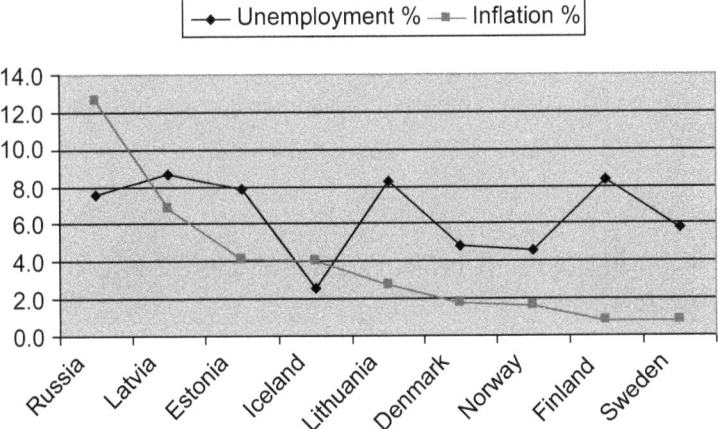

Fig. 8.2 Line graph

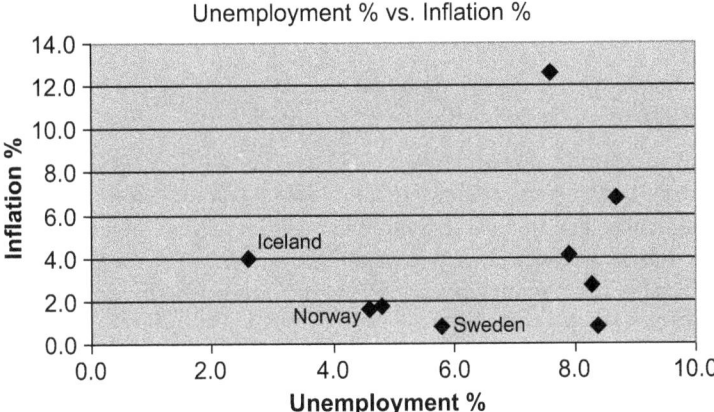

Fig. 8.3 Scatter diagram

Line graphs are another technique for visualizing data. They are particularly appropriate, when the order of alternatives has a special meaning as in time series. In Fig. 8.2, we ordered the countries (the alternatives) in terms of decreasing inflation rates. This should make it easier to see, how the unemployment rate and the inflation rate are related in different countries.

The dependence between the unemployment and the inflation rates can also be observed from the scatter diagram (Fig. 8.3). Figure 8.3 is also useful in case we are interested in recognizing the nondominated countries (in two dimensions): Iceland, Norway, and Sweden. They correspond to the South-Westernmost countries. Which country's economy is healthiest (in these two dimensions), depends on how we value low inflation vs. low unemployment.

Many other visualization techniques have been described in statistics textbooks, such as pie charts and boxplots, which may be useful in specific contexts. Pie charts are, for example, useful for visualizing probabilities and percentages. For further information, please consult any basic statistics book, such as Bowerman et al. (2004).

8.1.2 Visualization of Multivariate Data: More Advanced Techniques

Visual representation is limited to two (or three) dimensions. Therefore, the main problem in visualizing multivariate data is to construct a two-dimensional representation of it. A three-dimensional problem can be rather easily illustrated in two dimensions using standard techniques, but the ideas do not work for higher dimensional problems.

In statistics, two general principles have been applied for constructing a two-dimensional visual representation:

- Reduce the dimensionality of the problem or
- Plot a multivariate observation as an object (icon).

The aim in the dimensionality reduction is to decrease the dimensions of the problem without losing essential information. Principal component analysis (PCA) and multidimensional scaling (MDS) are two well-known techniques for obtaining such a two-dimensional representation of multivariate data. The reader is encouraged to consult Smith (2002) for a tutorial on PCA, and Everitt (1978) for visualization of multivariate data.

> **Example 8.1 Combining Criteria**
> As an example of the use of the principal component analysis, consider the situation, where the CEO of a bank group has information on five variables (criteria) for comparison purposes of individual banks under her supervision: Growth, Profitability, Debt, Solidity, and Investments. All these variables are relevant, but the CEO thinks that using fewer criteria might make comparison easier. None of those original criteria can be ignored, but principal component analysis finds new criteria by combining the original information into fewer criteria. The principal component analysis reveals that two first principal components explain 64.1% about information and three already 80.2%. Two or three (new) components make it possible to understand (summarize) how the banks are doing. (Tainio et al. 1991).

Multidimensional scaling (MDS) is another technique developed for dimension reduction. The purpose of MDS is to reduce the dimensionality of the problem with

8.1 Visual Representation of Numerical Data

Fig. 8.4 Radar chart

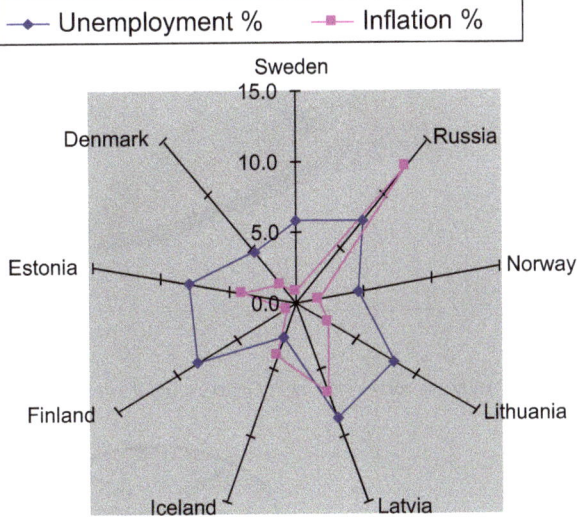

the aim of preserving the original distances of the alternatives in a lower (two) dimensional space to the extent possible.

In principle, some standard graphical techniques, such as bar charts and line graphs can be used to illustrate more than two- or three-variable data sets. When the number of variables and/or alternatives increases, the graphs, however, quickly become messy. In fact, so called radar charts are more appropriate to illustrate multivariate data, provided the number of variables is reasonably small. As you can see from Fig. 8.4, the radar chart is not very clear, even if we only have nine alternatives and two variables. However, the chart is understandable, if the number of variables is not large. A remedy to problems with a large number of variables is to represent them in different pictures.

In the early 1970s two interesting techniques: Andrews curves (Andrews 1972) and Chernoff faces (Chernoff 1973) were developed for visualizing multidimensional data. Andrews plotted each observation (alternative in MCDM lingo) as a harmonic curve, which is composed of sine- and cosine-functions (see Appendix). Thus, each observation is a curve in two dimensions. In this technique the number of variables is unlimited. The curves depend on the order in which the variables have been presented.

Figure 8.5 reproduces the famous iris flower data (R. Fisher 1936). The data set consists of three different species of iris flowers. This technique works best for clustering (grouping) data. For instance, from Fig. 8.5 we can see that all black curves have a quite similar form and they clearly differ from green and red curves. Instead, the red and green curves blend or overlap.

Chernoff used a human face to represent each observation (alternative) graphically. The construction of Chernoff faces consists of geometrically well-defined elements, such as arcs (segments) of circles, arcs of ellipses, and straight lines. They are used to describe the shape of the face, eyes and pupils, brows, nose and

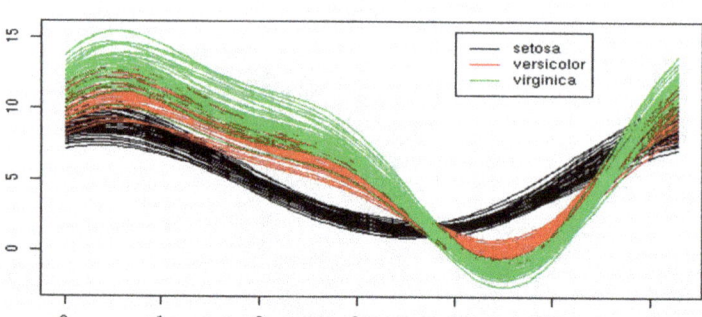

Fig. 8.5 Andrews curves (R Graph Gallery): Iris flower data

Fig. 8.6 Chernoff face

mouth. The values of variables are linked to the facial features. Chernoff's original proposal consisted of 18 face parameters (Fig. 8.6). Later other versions of the original face were developed.

Andrews harmonic curves and Chernoff faces help us view similarities and dissimilarities between observations, identify clusters, outliers etc., but they are not very good for conveying preference information. In Andrews curves, each curve stands for one observation, and the curves, which do not deviate much from each other, represent similar observations. In a Chernoff face, it is easy to understand that a "smile" means something positive, but the length of the nose does not convey similar information. In addition, we have no knowledge about the joint effects of the facial parameters. Big eyes and a long nose may make the face look silly in some user's mind (in some cultures), although big eyes are usually a positive feature.

In spite of the preceding disadvantages, the techniques provide us with new directions for developing visual techniques. Especially, there is a need for techniques, which can also convey preference information, in other words help us decide which alternative (picture) is best. Current developments in Artificial Intelligence (AI) and information technology (IT) perhaps in the near future provide solutions to the problem mentioned above. For instance, Chernoff's original idea can be further developed by replacing the cartoon-like face by realistic human faces. The number of variables (criteria) can be increased a lot and a human being can recognize small

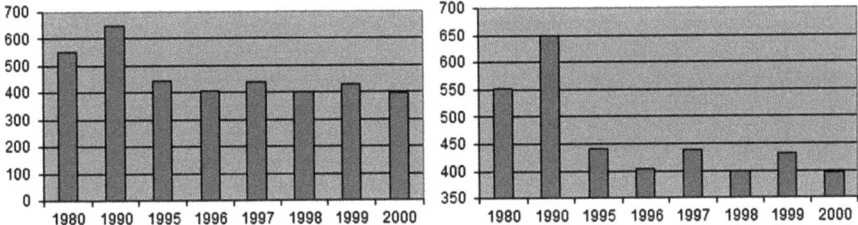

Fig. 8.7 Traffic fatalities in Finland: two representations

differences in facial features. We may also learn to recognize, which features together imply something positive and which something negative.

8.2 Lying with Graphs

We should always seek to present a truthful representation of the data. People, however, often on purpose or out of ignorance construct graphs that are misleading. One should always be aware of the ways statistical graphs and charts can be manipulated to distort the truth. We urge the reader to study the classic by Huff (1954): *How to Lie with Statistics*. In the multiple criteria framework, where a DM is an essential part of the solution process, this may be even more important. For example, when using an interactive decision support system, the DM is asked to react to graphical representations. A wrong illusion provided by the graph may lead to an undesirable final solution.

In the following, we present some common examples of (purposefully) misleading graphs. More can be found in Huff's book. In Fig. 8.7 we have described the development of traffic fatalities in Finland during select years between 1980–2000 using histograms. The left-hand figure stands for the standard case, where the vertical axis starts at zero. In the right-hand figure, we present the same data, but start the vertical axis at 350 instead of 0. This makes the decrease in traffic fatalities appear more dramatic.[2]

In Fig. 8.8, we illustrate the per capita electricity consumption in Denmark and Finland. The per capita electricity consumption in Finland is about twice that of Denmark's. It sounds an appealing idea to illustrate the electricity consumption by using an object somehow related to electricity, such as light bulbs. Maintaining the shape of the light bulb makes the electricity consumption (measured by the height of

---

[2]Interestingly, in Finland the traffic fatalities have continued to decrease. Today, their total number is about 200, despite the fact that the number of cars is much larger than in 1980, let alone 1960. This does not, however, change our recommendation that in graphs the y-axis should start at 0.

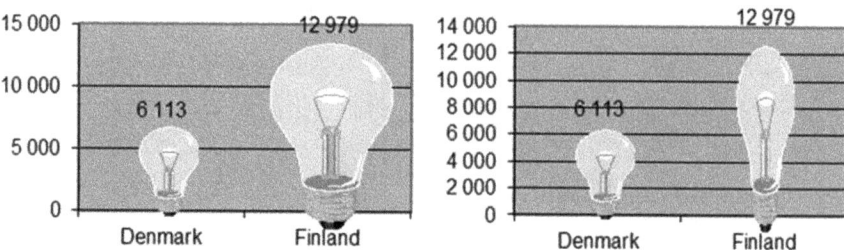

Fig. 8.8 Electricity consumption/capita in Denmark vs Finland

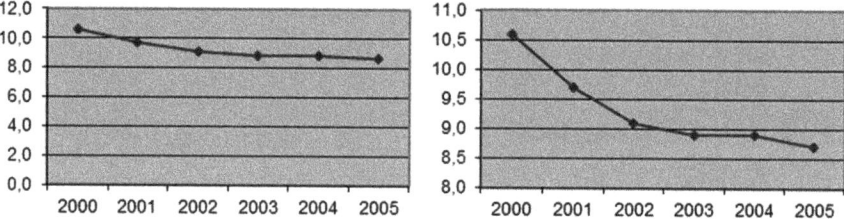

Fig. 8.9 Unemployment (%) in Finland during 2000–2005: two representations

the bulb) in Finland look much larger than it actually is in the left-hand figure. It is human that people compare the sizes of the bulbs instead of the height. In the right-hand figure, we have only stretched the height of Denmark's light bulb for Finland. The right-hand illustration provides a (more) correct impression.

In Fig. 8.9[3], we illustrate the outcome of stretching the y-axis. A neutral approach to describing, e.g., the development of the unemployment rate by using a line graph is to start the y-axis (percentage scale) from zero and end it above the maximum, as is done in the left-hand figure. If we stretch the y-axis and fix the range roughly from the minimum to the maximum, it makes the downward trend in unemployment rate look steeper in the right-hand figure, demonstrating "a dramatic improvement in the unemployment rate". This would obviously be in the interest of the government (back then).

---

[3]We do not wish to confuse the reader, but concerning the use of Figs 8.7, 8.8, and 8.9 in an MCDM context, it may sometimes be useful to zoom into some value range of objectives. This could be the case, when we like to compare small differences in objective values. However, usually a truthful, holistic picture is more desirable.

8.3 Visualization in Multiple Criteria Decision Support Systems

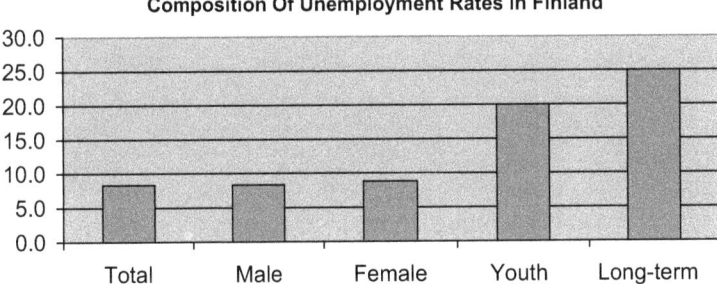

Fig. 8.10 Illustrating unemployment rates in different groups in Finland

8.3 Visualization in Multiple Criteria Decision Support Systems

When making choices between multi-criteria decision alternatives (in statistical lingo: multivariate data), the DMs can benefit from the use of graphical techniques described above. Such techniques may be used to provide the DM with holistic information and to obtain a quick overall view of the relevant information.

Graphical techniques have also been implemented as part of several man-computer systems developed for solving MCDM-problems. We briefly outline some of the graphical interfaces embedded in computer-based Decision Support Systems.

8.3.1 Snapshots of a Single Alternative

We can use graphical techniques to illustrate a single alternative. Techniques, such as bar charts, are suitable for this purpose, assuming that the number of criteria is not too large. The criteria are described on the x-axis and their values on the y-axis. Figure 8.10 illustrates unemployment rates in different population groups (male, female, youth) in Finland. One of the bars refers to long-term unemployment (as percentage of unemployed people). This corresponds to a situation of one alternative (Finland) and five criteria.

Chernoff faces (Fig. 8.6) is one of the techniques, which makes it possible to provide information on an alternative with one icon. In the MCDM context, one has multiple alternatives to choose from. Sometimes, the choice is between two (or a few) alternatives, sometimes the most preferred solution has to be chosen from a large number of alternatives. In the following subsection we consider these situations.

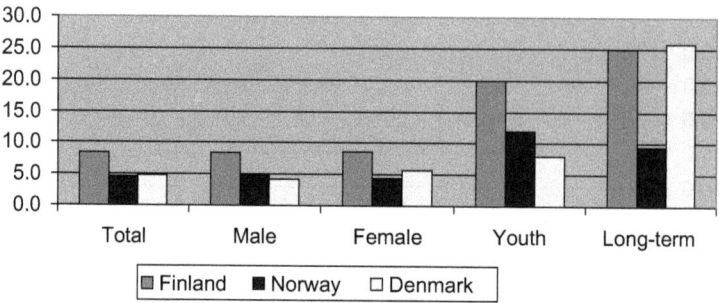

Fig. 8.11 Comparing unemployment rates in Finland, Norway, and Denmark

8.3.2 Illustrating a Set of Alternatives/Solutions

Bar charts, again, can be used to compare alternatives described with multiple criteria, when their number is small. In Fig. 8.11 we compare the unemployment rates using five sub-criteria in Finland, Norway and Denmark. In fact, one can think of Fig. 8.11 as consisting of three separate bar charts presented in one graph (to facilitate comparisons between countries). If one wants to choose the best country (in terms of various aspects of unemployment) from the three countries, it is difficult to conclude whether the unemployment situation in Norway was better than in Denmark (at the time of the picture). It depends on, how we weigh female vs. male unemployment, youth unemployment and long-term unemployment. (Finland is clearly the worst!)

A widely used alternative to bar charts in MCDM is to use line graphs. Each line commonly stands for one criterion. See Fig. 8.2 for a typical two-criteria example. The visual effect may be enhanced by ranking alternatives according to one criterion, as was done in Fig. 8.2.

A line graph may also be drawn in such a way that one line stands for one alternative; criteria are on the x-axis. In the MCDM framework, this is often called a score profile.

When standard graphical techniques (e.g. bar charts, value graphs, line graphs) are used to visualize alternatives, preference information is included in the details. Long bars, lines with a positive slope, etc. stand for good values or improvements. However, to obtain a holistic perception of these detailed pieces of preference information, is often impossible. Advanced techniques, such as Chernoff faces and Andrews harmonic curves help the DM obtain a holistic perception of the alternatives, but do not provide a good basis for the purpose of preference evaluation. In a later chapter, we discuss the underlying idea of 'harmonious' houses, a technique allowing preference comparisons between pictures (alternatives).

8.4 Why Visualization?

In this chapter we have considered the problem of visualizing multi-dimensional alternatives. The main purpose is to enable the DM to visually and holistically view multi-dimensional alternatives and facilitate preference comparisons. The alternatives may be presented one at a time, two at a time, or many at a time. Based on the available information, the MCDM-procedures ask the DM to choose the best (sometimes the worst) from the set of displayed alternatives, to rank, or to cluster alternatives. In many cases one can use standard statistical techniques, or their variations, developed for visualizing numerical data. In some cases, more advanced techniques, such as radar charts, Chernoff faces, and Andrews curves, are needed for visualizing alternatives.

Typically, the graphical representation is an essential part of the user interface in interactive Decision Support Systems. Such Decision Support Systems are discussed later in our book.

Appendix: Andrews Curves

Andrews (1972) curves were developed for visualizing multidimensional data by describing each observation $X_i = [x_{i1}, x_{i2}, \ldots, x_{ip}]$, $i = 1, 2, \ldots, n$, as a harmonic curve over the interval $-\pi \leq t \leq \pi$:

$$f_i(t) = \frac{x_{i1}}{\sqrt{2}} + x_{i2} \sin t + x_{i3} \cos t + x_{i4} \sin 2t + \ldots,$$

where p refers to the number of variables and n to the number of observations.

References

Andrews, D. (1972). Plots of high dimensional data. *Biometrics, 28*, 125–136.
Bowerman, B. L., O'Connell, R. T., & Orris, J. B. (2004). *Essentials in business statistics: Irwin series: Operations and decision sciences*. Boston, MA: McGraw-Hill.
Chernoff, H. (1973). Using faces to represent points in k-dimensional space graphically. *Journal of American Statistical Association, 68*, 361–368.
Everitt, B. (1978). *Graphical techniques for multivariate data*. London: Heinemann Educational Books.
Fisher, R. A. (1936). The use of multiple measurements in taxonomic problems. *Annual Eugenics, 7* (Part II), 179–188.
Huff, D. (1954). *How to lie with statistics*. New York: Norton.
Levine, D. M., Krehbiel, T. C., & Berenson, M. L. (2006). *Business statistics: A first course* (4th ed.). New Jersey: Prentice Hall.
R Graph Gallery. (n.d.). http://addictedtor.free.fr/graphiques/RGraphGallery.php?graph-=47, accessed 2020.

Smith, L. I. (2002). *A tutorial on principal components analysis*. Accessed from Internet http://www.cs.otago.ac.nz/cosc453/student_tutorials/principal_components.pdf

Tainio, R., Korhonen, P., & Santalainen, T. (1991). In search of explanations for bank performance – Finnish data. *Organization Studies, 12*(3), 425–450.

Chapter 9
Choosing Among Known Alternatives

We next discuss systematic approaches to solving so called multiple criteria evaluation problems. In this case, all decision alternatives are assumed to be known and available. Central to such approaches is the need to make tradeoffs. A classic example of a tradeoff is investing in stock market, where you must decide how much expected profits you desire and what risks you are willing to take. The higher risks you are willing to take, the higher is the potential payoff. However, we cannot achieve everything we desire, and we must make compromises.

We introduce one historical approach and three other approaches, which are based on different philosophies:

- Swapping the Values of Criteria (Even Swaps)
- Weighted Sums (The Analytic Hierarchy Process)
- Reference Direction Approach (VIMDA)

We start with a wonderful, over 200 years old Benjamin Franklin's approach. Then we discuss the "Even Swaps" approach, which is a modern version of the Benjamin Franklin's approach. The next approach we discuss is Tom Saaty's Analytic Hierarchy Process (AHP), perhaps the most popular approach among practitioners. We end the chapter with the description of the VIMDA approach, which is developed for problems having a large (even huge) number of alternatives, but just a few criteria.

Under Decision Support Systems we discuss some other approaches and their software implementations.

9.1 Benjamin Franklin's Approach

Benjamin Franklin (1706–1790) is known to most Americans. He was a statesman, scientist, inventor, and diplomat. He was one of the most influential founding fathers of the United States. As a young man, he developed a method for making complex decisions. He supposedly used his method also when facing complex decisions in government. In a letter to his friend, Joseph Priestley, written in London on September 19, 1772, Franklin described this method.

> In the affair of so much importance to you, wherein you ask my advice, I cannot for want of sufficient premises, advise you what to determine, but if you please I will tell you how. When these difficult cases occur, they are difficult chiefly because while we have them under consideration all the reasons pro and con are not present to the mind at the same time; but sometimes one set present themselves, and at other times another, the first being out of sight. Hence the various purposes or inclinations that alternately prevail, and the uncertainty that perplexes us. To get over this, my way is, to divide, half a sheet of paper by a line into two columns, writing over the one pro, and over the other con. Then during three or four day's consideration I put down under the different heads short hints of the different motives that at different times occur to me for or against the measure. When I have thus got them all together in one view, I endeavor to estimate their respective weights; and where I find two, one on each side, that seem equal, I strike them both out: if I find a reason pro equal to some two reasons con, I strike out the three. If I judge some two reasons con equal to some three reasons pro, I strike out the five; and thus proceeding I find at length where the balance lies; and if after a day or two of farther consideration nothing new that is of importance occurs on either side, I come to a determination accordingly. And though the weight of reasons cannot be taken with the precision of algebraic quantities, yet when each is thus considered separately and comparatively, and the whole lies before me, I think I can judge better, and am less likely to make a rash step; and in fact I have found great advantage from this kind of equation, in what may be called moral or prudential algebra. (Walter Isaacson, A Benjamin Franklin Reader, Isaacson 2003)

Making tradeoffs is notoriously difficult. The Benjamin Franklin's wonderful way of making tradeoffs can help. In fact, it served as the motivation for Hammond et al. (1998) article "Even Swaps" in Harvard Business Review some 200 years later. The more alternatives and criteria we are considering, the more tradeoffs we need to make. Some of them may be highly complex.

9.2 Even Swaps

The "Even Swaps" method forces us to think about the value of one criterion in terms of another. For a compensation of 300 euros, would you get off an overbooked plane and fly next morning? The authors warn that their method does not make tradeoffs easy, but it provides a systematic mechanism for making them.

Before making tradeoffs, we need to structure the problem. We need to list the alternatives and the consequences for each decision-relevant criterion, resulting in a table (consequences table). Note that some of the consequences may be expressed as numbers, some qualitatively (using words). We illustrate the consequences table for

9.2 Even Swaps

Table 9.1 Consequences table (Original)

Criteria/Jobs	A	B	C	D
1. Monthly salary	6000	4500	8000	5500
2. Job flexibility	Great	Good	Fair	Great
3. Enjoyment	Good	Good	Good	Great
4. Independence	Great	Good	Fair	Great
5. Future career	Good/Great	Fair	Fair	Great

the problem of a young PhD deciding among several job offers. The table itself is useful, because it forces us to list all available alternatives, all decision-relevant criteria, and their consequences. This task is not trivial.

Job A: A tenure track assistant professor's position in a business school in a Finnish university (located in mid-Finland) in the applicant's field of expertise
Job B: A tenured lecturer's position in a major Helsinki metropolitan university
Job C: A job as an analyst in a large IT company located in Helsinki metropolitan area
Job D: A tenure track assistant professor's position in a major university in Helsinki metropolitan area, however in an engineering school

The candidate is interested in pursuing an academic career. Her PhD is from a business school. Given that her home is in Helsinki, the 'rural' university is not ideal, but not excluded. The candidate does not have a family. The lecturer's position is with tenure, both of the assistant professor's positions would be 6-year contracts, after which the candidate would be evaluated for tenure and promotion to Associate Professorship. The lecturer's position would imply twice the teaching load compared to the two assistant professor's positions. Job C would be a relatively well-paying company job. Not ideal, considering her academic ambitions, but it would not be excluded to work in a company for a couple of years after graduation.

The decision-relevant criteria are the following:

1. Monthly salary (euros)
2. Job flexibility
3. Enjoyment
4. Independence
5. Helping with future career prospects in academia

Let us first see if we can find any dominated alternatives. In fact, job B is dominated by A and D, because in terms of each criterion it is either worse or equally good than A or D. Hence there is no need to consider job B further, and column B can be eliminated from the Consequences Table (Table 9.1). Sometimes dominance is not as easy to detect. If we replace the verbal descriptions (great, good, fair) with rankings, dominance is easier to detect.

We are left with three non-dominated alternatives (jobs): A, C, and D. They each have pros and cons. C's pay is highest, but it has some serious cons. Jobs A and D are rather similar. A has a better pay, but D is better in terms of enjoyment, and has the potential to better further her (academic) career.

Table 9.2 Consequences table (Reduced)

Criteria/Jobs	A	C	D
1. Monthly salary	**5000**	**7000**	5500
2. Job flexibility	Great	Fair	Great
3. Enjoyment	*Great*	*Great*	Great
4. Independence	Good/Great	Fair	Great
5. Future career	Good/Great	Fair	Great

Next, think about the enjoyment criterion. Jobs A and C are good in terms of this criterion, but D is great. A and D are both academic jobs, but D is in her home town, close to most of her friends and relatives; hence providing great enjoyment. Let us think, how much she would be willing to pay (that is, compromise in monthly salary), to change enjoyment from good to great (marked italics in Table 9.2). Let us assume that her response is 1000 euros. Let us make the following change in the consequences table: change enjoyment values for jobs A and C to great. At the same time, reduce the monthly salary of A from 6000 to 5000, and of C from 8000 to 7000 (marked bold in Table 9.2). We call this an even swap. Accordingly, all the criterion values for enjoyment are equal, and the enjoyment criterion can be deleted.

By comparing jobs A and D, we note that D dominates the updated A, leaving us with two non-dominated jobs, C and D. In C, values for criteria 2, 4, and 5 are all fair, compared to great in job D. The salary difference between C and D is 1500 (per month). The question is, whether 1500 more in salary would compensate for great job flexibility, independence, and the difference in future academic prospects. It would seem that choosing job C would be for money. The choice between C and D eventually boils down between an academic, tenure-track position and a company position. If the person wants to pursue an academic career, then our advice for her would be to take job D.

In a nutshell, the even swaps are used for eliminating criteria; dominance is for eliminating alternatives. If you do both, the problem (the Consequences Table) quickly simplifies.

9.3 Weighted Sums

9.3.1 Weights and Scales

The most common way to "solve" evaluation problems in practice is to construct the consequences table showing the alternatives as rows and the criteria as columns. If the criteria are readily presented on the same "scale", then for each alternative we often calculate a score by computing the weighted sum of the criteria. As weights we use numbers, which stand for "importance" of the criteria.

We have embedded the words "solve", "scale", and "importance" in quotation marks, because they require a more precise description. We illustrate with an example dealing with buying a car. The data for the example is from the Finnish

9.3 Weighted Sums

Table 9.3 Basic data for the car buying example

Car	Price €	D:1 G:0	Engine cm^3	Max speed km/h	Fuel cons. l/100 km	Warranty # of years	CO$_2$-Emiss. g/km
Seat Tarraco	37,645	1	1968	210	7.3	5	191
Porsche Macan	84,967	1	1984	225	10	2	227
Citroën Berlingo	22,339	1	1499	185	5.7	3	151
BMW 840D	141,003	1	2993	250	7	2	186
Lexus ES	49,218	0	2487	180	5.3	3	120
Nissan Qashqai	28,620	0	1332	193	5.7	3	161
Suzuki	23,990	0	998	180	7.8	3	176

Magazine Moottori (Motor) published by the Automobile and Touring Club of Finland (ATCF) (Table 9.3).

We have selected seven new cars, which we evaluate using seven attributes: Price (list price), Diesel (1) vs. Gasoline (0), the Size of Engine (cm^3), Max Speed (km/h), Fuel Consumption (liters/100 km), Warranty (years), and CO$_2$-emissions (g/km). Let us assume (even though this might not sound very realistic) that we have decided to buy a car from the list of seven cars, using seven criteria. The criteria have been constructed from the attributes.

First, we specify importance weights for the criteria as follows: for price 5, Diesel vs Gas 3, Engine size 4, Max Speed 3, Fuel Consumption 5, Warranty 4, and CO$_2$-Emissions 4. Note, however, that it makes no sense to use the weights for the original attributes, because, for instance, Price multiplied by five is of different magnitude compared to the weighted values of other attributes. We first need to introduce a value scale for each attribute.

We also need to specify, whether the criteria are of 'maximizing' or 'minimizing' type, in other words, whether more is preferable to less, or the other way. Smaller values are preferred for Price, Fuel Consumption, and CO$_2$-emissions. For other attributes, more is preferred to less. Note that since we defined Diesel $= 1$, and Gas $= 0$, diesel cars would be preferable to gasoline cars.

We have to find a reasonable way to scale (or transform) the values of the attributes, so that it would be meaningful to operate with weighted sums. We call the transformed attribute a criterion scale. There are many ways to make the transformation. For demonstrating the importance of the connection between weights and scales, we present three ways:

1. We interpret the weight as the value (utility) of the best score (to the DM), and we would like to preserve the ratios of the values of each attribute. This means that in case of maximization, we divide the values of each attribute by the best (largest) value of the attribute. Thus, the transformed best value of each attribute becomes 1.

Table 9.4 Ranking the cars, using Way 1 to scale the attributes

Car type	Price €	D(1)/ G(0)	Eng. cm³	Max speed km/h	Cons. l/ 100 km	Warranty # of years	CO₂-Emiss. g/km	Value
Weights	5	3	4	3	5	4	4	
Citroën Berlingo	1.00	1.00	0.50	0.74	0.93	0.60	0.79	22.5
Seat Tarraco	0.59	1.00	0.66	0.84	0.73	1.00	0.63	21.3
Lexus ES	0.45	0.00	0.83	0.72	1.00	0.60	1.00	19.2
BMW 840D	0.16	1.00	1.00	1.00	0.76	0.40	0.65	18.8
Nissan Qashqai	0.78	0.00	0.45	0.77	0.93	0.60	0.75	18.0
Suzuki	0.93	0.00	0.33	0.72	0.68	0.60	0.68	16.7
Porsche Macan	0.26	1.00	0.66	0.90	0.53	0.40	0.53	16.0

2. The best value is as in 1, but we would stretch the scale in such a way that the worst value is 0.
3. We scale each attribute in such a way that the sum of the transformed values is 1. This would preserve the ratios of the values of each attribute.

We illustrate the three ways of scaling an attribute value with a simple example. Assume three alternatives A, B, and C, which are evaluated with one attribute to be maximized, such that $A = 10$, $B = 8$, and $C = 2$ represent the three alternatives. The new scales are computed as follows:

$$\text{Way 1}: (10, 8, 2) \rightarrow \left(\frac{10}{10}, \frac{8}{10}, \frac{2}{10}\right) = (1, 0.8, 0.2)$$

$$\text{Way 2}: (10, 8, 2) \rightarrow \left(\frac{10-2}{10-2}, \frac{8-2}{10-2}, \frac{2-2}{10-2}\right) = (1, 0.75, 0)$$

$$\text{Way 3}: (10, 8, 2) \rightarrow \left(\frac{10}{10+8+2}, \frac{8}{10+8+2}, \frac{2}{10+8+2}\right) = (0.5, 0.4, 0.1)$$

Ways 1 and 3 are reasonable only if all values are positive. The example was based on the assumption that the attribute in question was maximized. In case of minimization, we use the opposite values of the attributes.

We demonstrate how the different scalings affect the rankings in our car example, when the given weights are used for the transformed scale values.

As you can see, all rankings are different. The only difference between rankings in Tables 9.4 and 9.5 is that Seat Tarraco and Citroën Berlingo have changed their places. This might be very essential, if we would have used the system to choose the best car. In Table 9.6, we see that BMW 840D is ranked three positions lower than in

9.3 Weighted Sums

Table 9.5 Ranking the cars, using Way 2 to scale the attributes

Car type	Price €	D(1)/ G(0)	Eng. cm^3	Max speed km/h	Cons. l/ 100 km	Warranty # of years	CO$_2$-Emiss. g/km	Value
Weights	5	3	4	3	5	4	4	
Seat Tarraco	0.87	1.00	0.49	0.43	0.57	1.00	0.34	18.8
Citroën Berlingo	1.00	1.00	0.25	0.07	0.91	0.33	0.71	18.0
Lexus ES	0.77	0.00	0.75	0.00	1.00	0.33	1.00	17.2
BMW 840D	0.00	1.00	1.00	1.00	0.64	0.00	0.38	14.7
Nissan Qashqai	0.95	0.00	0.17	0.19	0.91	0.33	0.62	14.3
Suzuki	0.99	0.00	0.00	0.00	0.47	0.33	0.48	10.5
Porsche Macan	0.47	1.00	0.49	0.64	0.00	0.00	0.00	9.3

Table 9.6 Ranking the cars, using Way 3 to scale the attributes

Car type	Price €	D(1)/ G(0)	Eng. cm^3	Max speed km/h	Cons. l/ 100 km	Warranty # of years	CO$_2$-Emiss. g/km	Value
Weights	−5	3	4	3	−5	4	−4	
Seat Tarraco	0.09	0.25	0.12	0.13	0.13	0.19	0.14	0.67
Citroën Berlingo	0.05	0.25	0.09	0.11	0.11	0.12	0.11	0.66
Lexus ES	0.12	0.00	0.15	0.11	0.10	0.12	0.09	−0.05
Nissan Qashqai	0.07	0.00	0.08	0.12	0.11	0.12	0.12	−0.22
Suzuki	0.06	0.00	0.06	0.11	0.14	0.12	0.13	−0.51
BMW 840D	0.34	0.25	0.18	0.15	0.13	0.08	0.14	−0.68
Porsche Macan	0.21	0.25	0.12	0.13	0.18	0.08	0.17	−0.69

the previous tables. In each table, Porsche Macan is the least desirable choice. However, this kind of analysis does not necessarily do justice to Porsche Macan.

The lesson from above is that you have to understand the mutual relationship between the weights and the scales of the criteria. It is also very important that you have a clear idea what you mean with the importance weights. How have they been derived? It is also a good idea that you try a bit different set of weights just to see how robust (or sensitive) the ranking is to the exact weights. In the above example, it seems that the DM has grouped the seven criteria into three classes of importance: the most important criteria (assigned a weight 5), the second most important criteria (assigned a weight 4), and the least important criteria (assigned a weight 3).

To a human being it seems easy to "softly" evaluate the mutual importance of various criteria. If you ask somebody, which is more important to you "more salary" or "more leisure time", most people immediately offer you a response, without questioning the fuzziness of the question. Perhaps the person has in her mind a certain, realistic salary increase (say 500 euros per month), and a realistic increase in leisure (say 3 days in a year). By, for example stating that the salary increase is more important than the increase in leisure, you are in fact stating that it is more important to you to get a 500-euro salary increase versus three additional vacation days. The problem is that we do not know, what salary increase and what increase in vacation days the person has in mind. You may observe the same ambiguity in the speeches of politicians, when they discuss, for example, the importance of decreasing inflation versus unemployment. Each politician has some mental model regarding the trade-off options in their head, but definitely it is not the same for everybody. And the tradeoff is seldom made transparent.

9.4 Beware of Joint Effects of Similar Criteria

Now we show how the joint effects of similar criteria may lead to a completely different solution, what we initially had in mind. Assume that you compare various places for spending your summer holidays. You would like to find a budget place with good possibilities for various recreational activities. You are interested in hiking, fishing, hunting, swimming, and surfing. Moreover, assume price is very important to you. You specify the following weights for your criteria: nine for price (best value for the cheapest holidays) and two for each activity criterion. It means that price is 4.5 times more important than any of the activities.

You have explored potential candidates and found the following three:

- A is the cheapest place (best score 10), but activity possibilities are poor (the worst score 1 for each activity)
- B is quite cheap (5), and the activity possibilities are OK (5), and
- C is expensive (the worst score 1), but all activity possibilities are excellent (best 10).

Because price is important to you, you give it a weight 9, and a weight 2 for all the other activities. So! What do you get, when you compute the weighted sums? Your Decision Support System offers you alternative C as the best (the total score is 109). Perhaps this is not quite what you meant. Alternative B can never be the best, no matter which weights you use! B falls in the "hole of mediocrity". Depending on the weights, A or C is always better.

The point with this example is that we have many similar criteria (activities). Because none of the five activities per se is very important, we give a low weight for each of them. However, their joint effect is significant. One way to overcome this problem is to build a hierarchy of criteria in such a way that you have two main

Table 9.7 Choosing a place for holidays

Place	Price	Hiking	Fishing	Hunting	Swimming	Surfing	Sum
	9	2	2	2	2	2	
A	10	1	1	1	1	1	100
B	5	5	5	5	5	5	95
C	1	10	10	10	10	10	109

Table 9.8 Choosing the best alternative by restricting criterion values

Machine	Price ($)	Washing time	Electricity consumption	Water consumption
1	509	74	1.5	114
2	395	76	1.5	120
3	564	65	1.6	118
4	536	57	1.7	110
5	488	72	1.6	114
6	543	57	1.6	120
7	534	61	1.4	122

criteria: price and 'activities' (lumped together). Next you would take a closer look at the different activity criteria (Table 9.7).[1]

9.5 Do Not Accidentally Eliminate the Best Alternative!

Next, we illustrate how setting restrictions for different criterion levels may lead to a non-satisfactory outcome. This approach is not uncommon among practitioners. We use a subset (seven alternatives) from Milan Zeleny's washing machine example, which originally consisted of 33 machines (Table 9.8).

Price is the most important criterion for our DM. However, assume that she is not willing to accept a too long washing time, and specifies that at most 70 min is acceptable. (To simplify, we assume that the washing machines only have one cycle.) Thus alternatives 1, 2, and 5 are eliminated from further consideration. She eliminated the cheapest alternative (#2), even though she hardly meant that.

This kind of accidental elimination may happen very easily. If you are choosing a flat, you may initially specify that you want a four-bedroom flat. By setting a four-bedroom restriction, you are not considering three-bedroom dream flats which might very well be within your budget.

---

[1] If you are a member in a group, which is searching for the best alternative by using a similar table as Table 9.7, you can propose several new criteria to support your proposal. It may help you 'win' the negotiation.

9.6 The Analytic Hierarchy Process

The Analytic Hierarchy Process (AHP) is a systematic approach to analyzing complex decisions. It is designed for problems where we know the decision alternatives. It was originally developed by Thomas L. Saaty in the 1970s (Saaty 1982). It is one of the most popular decision-making approaches used by practitioners all over the world. Rather than finding an 'optimal' decision, it helps decision-makers to find a solution that best suits their goals. It also helps decision-makers understand what they want.

The AHP decomposes the problem into a hierarchy of several smaller, independent subproblems. On top of the hierarchy is the overall goal. The next layer consists of the main criteria. Each of the main criteria may further be decomposed into sub-criteria. At the bottom of the hierarchy are the alternatives.

Once the hierarchy has been built, the decision-makers evaluate its various elements by comparing them to each other two at a time, with respect to their impact on an element which lies above them in the hierarchy.

Decision-makers typically use subjective judgments about the relative importance of each element. The AHP asks the decision-maker to make pairwise comparisons using the following relative importance scale:

1 = Equal importance
3 = Moderate importance of one over the other
5 = Essential or strong importance
7 = Very strong importance
9 = Extreme importance
2, 4, 6, and 8 represent intermediate values.

You are expected to (pairwise) compare each (main) criterion against each other. If there are sub-criteria, you are expected to compare the sub-criteria against each other (separately for each main criterion). Finally, you compare (again, pairwise) how well each alternative contributes towards each criterion.

The information contained in the pairwise comparisons is synthesized by deriving a numerical weight for each element (criterion, alternative) representing its relative importance. We illustrate with an example.

Let us consider our job selection problem that we discussed in connection with the Even Swaps approach. Let us, however, simplify the problem so that we ignore alternative B (the remaining alternatives are A, C, and D), and also ignore criteria 2 and 3 (the remaining criteria are 1, 4, and 5).

Let us first elicit the pairwise comparisons for the three remaining criteria. Assume that (using Saaty's scale) criteria 4 and 5 are 2-times more important than criterion 1, and that criterion 5 is 3-times more important than criterion 4. Based on these pairwise comparisons, we form the following Table 9.9:

This is how we read the table. The diagonal consists of 1 s (comparing a criterion with itself). In rows 4 and 5, column 1, the value indicates that criteria 4 and 5 are 2-times more important than criterion 1. Note that correspondingly the elements in row 1 and columns 4 and 5 are ½, implying that criteria 4 and 5 are two-times as

9.6 The Analytic Hierarchy Process

Table 9.9 Pairwise comparison of criteria

Criteria	1	4	5
1	1	1/2	1/2
4	2	1	1/3
5	2	3	1

Table 9.10 Comparison of jobs for criterion 5

Jobs	A	C	D
A	1	5	1/2
C	1/5	1	1/5
D	2	5	1

important as criterion 1. Next, we synthesize the pairwise comparison information into relative importance weights for the criteria. To do that calculate the product of the three numbers in each row. This leads to ¼ for the first criterion (row), 2/3 for the 4th criterion, and 6 for the 5th criterion. Next, take the third root of each of these three values. The third root of ¼ is 0.63, of 2/3 it is 0.87, and of 6 it is 1.82. Next, let us normalize the three values so that they add up to 1. We can do this by adding: $0.63 + 0.87 + 1.82 = 3.32$; and dividing 0.63 by 3.32 (0.19), 0.87 by 3.32 (0.26), and 1.82 by 3.32 (0.55). The 5th criterion receives the highest importance with its 55% weight. The 1st criterion is least important, with a weight of 19%.

Next, we need to construct three such 3 by 3 tables (matrices), telling us how each job alternative (relatively) contributes towards each criterion. To illustrate, let us do that for criterion 5 (Table 9.10):

In other words, job A is considered (by us) 5-times better than job C in terms of this criterion; D is 2-times as good as job A, etc. By repeating the process of taking the third root of the product of the numbers in each row, we get the following priorities (how well each job contributes towards the 5th criterion): job $A = 20\%$, job $C = 0.3\%$, job $D = 80\%$.

To save space, we do not provide the pairwise comparison tables for criteria 1 and 4. However, we will provide for the reader's benefit, the priority vectors (based on our subjective pairwise comparison table), telling us how well each job contributes towards these criteria:

Criterion 1: $A = 2\%$, $C = 98\%$, $D = 0.4\%$
Criterion 4: $A = 49.8\%$, $C = 0.4\%$, $D = 49.8\%$

Once we have the priority weights for all the criteria, we can synthesize the information. For each job separately, we simply multiply the weights of the criteria with the relative weight, how well each job does with respect to that specific criterion. We illustrate for job A:

0.02 times 0.19 + 0,498 times 0.262 + 0.20 times 0.548 = 0.24

Similarly, the aggregate number for job $C = 0.19$, and for $D = 0.57$. Hence, based on the analysis (and the subjective preference information provided), job D would be most preferable.

9.6.1 Formulating a Marketing Strategy for a Small IT Company

We used the AHP to formulate a marketing strategy for one of the products of a small Finnish software company that we were involved with.[2] The company was originally founded to market self-made microcomputer-based Decision Support Systems. The systems represented the latest state-of-the art in MCDM at the time.

We considered the following strategies:

1. Sell on demand
2. Direct marketing efforts to academic colleagues abroad
3. Direct marketing efforts to Finnish colleagues
4. Direct marketing efforts to foreign companies
5. Direct marketing efforts to Finnish companies
6. Develop a retailer network
7. Advertising in management magazines abroad
8. Advertise in management magazines in Finland
9. Create publicity via publishing in scholarly journals

We formulated the following objectives, all to be maximized (except for the fifth objective):

1. Short-term profits
2. Long-term profits
3. Enjoyment
4. Academic prestige
5. Minimum workload

The hierarchy was simple in this case. The first layer consisted of the five objectives, and the second layer of the nine strategies. Arrows would connect each strategy with each objective. Note that we did not define units for the objectives. We used the AHP to figure out the contribution (or influence) of each strategy towards each objective. We did this objective by objective and made pairwise comparisons, such as how many more times is strategy 1 better than strategy 2 when considering short-term profits, etc. The outcome was a table, where each row (objective) summed to 100 points.

Table 9.11 tells us that strategy 2 (Direct marketing efforts to academic colleagues abroad) contributes best to objective 1 (Short-term profits). Strategy 6 (Develop a retailer network) contributes best to objective 2 (Long-term profits). Strategy 9 contributes best to objectives 3 (Enjoyment) and 4 (Academic prestige). Strategies 1 and 2 contribute best to objective five.

We used our VIG software to solve for the Most Preferred Solution. It was in terms of strategies:

---

[2]This was before the internet era.

Table 9.11 Outcome table: marketing strategy

O/S	1	2	3	4	5	6	7	8	9
1	2.2	34	10	5	9	14	3	6	16
2	2	19	3	8	4	36	11	7	10
3	18	16	7	5	2	12	3	2	36
4	2	17	5	7	3	6	15	4	41
5	33	6	28	3	6	8	3	6	8

Key: Rows = objectives; columns = strategies (Source: Korhonen and Wallenius 1990)

- Strategy 2 (Direct marketing efforts to academic colleagues abroad) = 0.14
- Strategy 6 (Develop a retailer network) = 0.30
- Strategy 9 (Create publicity via publishing in scholarly journals) = 0.56

The numbers should be interpreted as relative efforts.

In the optimal solution, we would weigh the objectives as follows: objective 1 = 18, objective 2 = 19, objective 3 = 26, objective 4 = 27, objective 5 = 8 (some rounding). Having fun and academic prestige were the most important objectives for us in the endeavor.

9.7 Visual Interactive Method for Discrete Alternatives (VIMDA)

Even Swaps and the Analytic Hierarchy Process are very suitable to decision-makers who need help solving problems consisting of a few alternatives and many criteria—sometimes with a hierarchical structure. However, they are not applicable to solving problems with a large (even huge) number (> 1,000,000) of alternatives, which are evaluated with a moderate number of criteria (say, at most 10). VIMDA is a method developed and published by Pekka Korhonen (1988) for such large-scale problems. The author also developed the first computer system embedding VIMDA. The current (and much more user-friendly) system has been developed by Jyri Ruutu together with the author.

The basic idea in VIMDA is that the search for the Most Preferred Solution (or alternative) is all the time in the hands of the DM. The DM specifies which kind of alternatives interest her and the system generates such alternatives for the DM's evaluation. A step-by-step description of the procedure follows:

1. Find a nondominated alternative to start the search.
2. Ask the DM to tell which criterion values she wants to improve, defining an aspiration point.
3. VIMDA generates a direction (called a reference direction) starting from the current alternative and passing through the virtual aspiration point.
4. The reference direction is projected onto the set of non-dominated alternatives. This set (called a projected set) is provided to the DM for her evaluation using a

Fig. 9.1 Illustration of the Main Idea of VIMDA

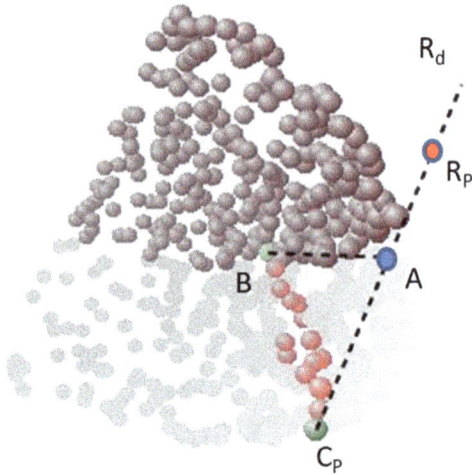

graphical interface (see Chap. 12). Each point in this set is the "closest point" to the direction at a certain stage.

5. The DM is asked to choose the most preferred alternative from the set of alternatives. Name this alternative the current alternative. The search continues as long as the DM is willing to give a new aspiration point for any of the criteria; otherwise, stop.

The procedure is illustrated in Fig. 9.1.

The current alternative is marked by C_p. The virtual alternative (aspiration point) reflecting the DM's desire to improve the criterion values of alternative C_p is marked by R_p. The dotted line starting from C_p and passing through R_p is the reference direction, which is projected onto the set of non-dominated alternatives (dark grey). In Fig. 9.1, we illustrate the situation, in which we have "walked" from C_p to B, and the light red balls stand for the projection of line from C_p to A. For each light grey ball, there exists a red ball which is closer to the line. Thus, the light grey balls are eliminated from further analysis. The projection of point A is B (marked green).

The projection process continues by providing a new aspiration point, a new reference direction, and its projection.

Each projection phase takes only a few seconds even for quite a large data set. Thus, the DM is able to make several iterations within a reasonable time limit.

References

Hammond, J., Keeney, R., & Raiffa, H. (1998). Even swaps: A rational method for making tradeoffs. *Harvard Business Review, 76*(2), 137–149.
Isaacson, W. (2003). *A Benjamin Franklin Reader*. New York: Simon & Schuster.

References

Korhonen, P. (1988). A visual reference direction approach to solving discrete multiple criteria problems. *European Journal of Operational Research, 34*, 152–159.

Korhonen, P., & Wallenius, J. (1990). Using qualitative data in multiple objective linear programming. *European Journal of Operational Research, 48*(1), 81–87.

Saaty, T. L. (1982). *Decision making for leaders: The analytical hierarchy process for decisions in a complex world.* Belmont, CA: Lifetime Learning.

Chapter 10
Designing Potential Solutions

Thus far, we have discussed decision-making in the framework, where all decision alternatives are known or can be enumerated. In that case, the problem is to identify the most preferred alternative from among those alternatives.

The other kind of problem is referred to as the 'design' problem. In that framework the decision alternatives are defined with the help of constraints (mathematical restrictions), as was briefly discussed in Chap. 7. Alternatives, which satisfy all restrictions, define feasible alternatives (or the feasible set). There are infinitely many such alternatives. The problem is to choose the most preferred alternative. How to do that is not trivial. Obviously, the decision-maker needs help in this process. There are many approaches to solving such multiple criteria design problems. In this chapter we discuss the fundamental concepts of the design problem, and one representative approach for solving such problems.

10.1 Feasible Set and Nondominated Set for the Design Problem

We illustrate the fundamental ideas for formulating and solving design problems by using two-criteria (or objective) representations. With them we can illustrate the main ideas, but at the expense of many important details. In the context of the 'design' problem, alternatives are usually referred to as solutions, and criteria as objectives.

Throughout this chapter, we use the following example:

Example 10.1 Tennis-Billiard Example
Assume that James would like to spend part of his day-off playing billiard[1] and/or tennis. How can we help James decide how many hours to play billiard and/or tennis? How to approach the problem?

We use capital letters B and T to refer to the hours he spends playing tennis and billiard, respectively. It is not uncommon to specify various constraints involving B and T. We will show how. Let us assume that the maximal number of hours for these two activities is eight. Accordingly, we specify mathematically that: $T + B \leq 8$ (the area below line I in Fig. 9.1). Moreover, it is not realistic to assume that James could play tennis more than 6 h the same day, because tennis is physically so demanding (although there would be 8 h available). Moreover, James thinks that if he plays 3 h of billiard that would diminish his capacity to play tennis by 1 h. Hence, we set an additional constraint: $T + \frac{1}{3}B \leq 6$ (the area below line II). James has also decided to spend at least 3 h playing tennis or billiard or both: $T + B \geq 3$ (the area above line III). Likewise, he does not want to spend more than 6 h playing billiard: $B \leq 6$ (the area to left from line IV).

When we combine all these four conditions (constraints) and add nonnegativity constraints (you cannot play tennis or billiard a negative number of hours), the set of possible solutions, which satisfies all constraints, is the shaded area in Fig. 10.1. This area consists of all feasible solutions and any point in this area (e.g., $T = 2$ and $B = 4$; i.e. point Q_1 in Fig. 10.1) is a possible (feasible) solution of the problem.

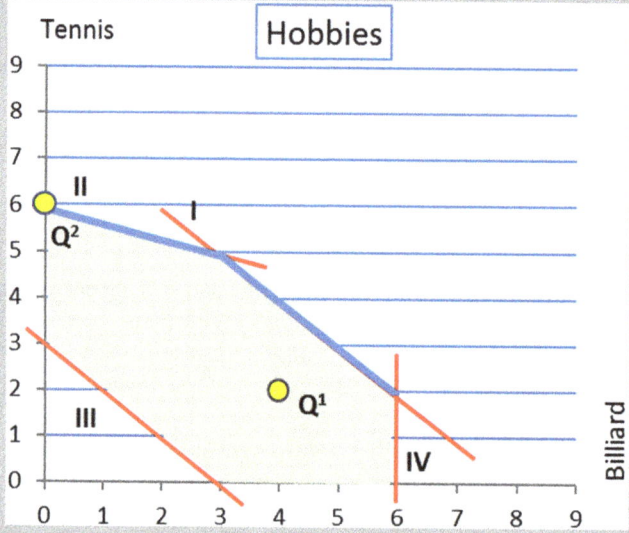

Fig. 10.1 The feasible and nondominated set of Example 10.1

(continued)

---

[1]Often the plural form 'billiards' is used. The game is called 'pool' in the US.

10.1 Feasible Set and Nondominated Set for the Design Problem

Example 10.1 (continued)

Because James has not specified precisely what he really wants, all feasible solutions are equally good (for now). How can James specify what he wants? We normally start by stating objectives (to be maximized or minimized). Let us assume that James does the same. In other words, he states his objectives. If playing tennis is his only objective (to be maximized), the optimal solution is clearly $B = 0$ and $T = 6$ (point Q^2 Fig. 10.1). In this situation, James would only be interested in having the best possible value for T (=maximal hours for playing tennis) subject to all constraints.

If James would like to play both tennis and billiard as much as possible, then there exists no optimal solution for the problem without additional preference information. Without such preference information, we can only say that any solution, which lies on the two blue line segments[2] in Fig. 10.1 is reasonable (nondominated) for the problem.

If we choose any point on the blue line segments in Fig. 10.1, there is no other point in the feasible set (the shaded area), which would provide us with more time for tennis and billiards. In other words, we cannot go north-east from the blue line segments and stay feasible. Next, consider solution $B = 4$ and $T = 2$ (point Q^1). This solution is dominated by, for example, $B = 4.5$ and $T = 2.5$, which is feasible and better than Q^1 in terms of both B and T.

Without any preference information from James, all solutions on the nondominated (blue) line segments are possibly best. Any choice from the nondominated line segments is rational. However, choosing, e.g., point Q_1, for which we can find better solutions in terms of both objectives, is not rational (wise). Please note that even though solutions on the blue line segments are rational, this does not mean that James would not have preferences (possibly strong preferences) among rational (nondominated) solutions.

Mathematically, the problem is presented as follows:

max T
max B

subject to

$T + B \leq 8$,
$T + \frac{1}{3}B \leq 6$,
$T + B \geq 3$,
$B \leq 6$,
$T \geq 0$,
$B \geq 0$.

The above problem is a Multiple Objective Linear Programming problem, and the abbreviation MOLP is used to refer to such problems. Because the number of

---

[2]The nondominated set is called a nondominated frontier.

objectives is only two, we may also call it a bi-objective Linear Programming problem.

The bi-objective Linear Programming problem is very simple, because the non-dominated set is generally composed of several line segments (the blue line segments in Fig. 10.1). To help the DM find her most preferred (best) solution, it is enough to let the DM visually look at the solutions on the non-dominated piecewise linear curve, make note of the numerical values of both objectives, and choose the Most Preferred Solution.

When the MOLP-problem has three objectives, it is still possible to solve the problem by combining visual and numerical representations. However, in case of more than three objectives, advanced methods are needed to help the DM find her Most Preferred Solution.

In the following, we introduce the reader to a historical approach called Goal Programming, dating back to the 1950s, to solving MOLP-problems. See Gass and Assad (2005) for the history of Operations Research, including Goal Programming.

10.2 Goal Programming

Charnes, Cooper and Ferguson proposed the use of Goal Programming as a way to deal with multiple objectives in the 'design' framework already in 1955. See also the famous book by Charnes and Cooper (1961). Since then Goal Programming has been an active field of research. Some of the early textbooks have been written by Lee (1972) and Ignizio (1976). Goal Programming has also been widely applied to solving practical problems.

We illustrate the basic idea of Goal Programming with Example 10.2 which is a continuation to Example 10.1.

> **Example 10.2 Tennis-Billiard Example Revisited**
> Assume that James would like to use Goal Programming to find the best solution to his problem. James starts by defining goal values for the hours he would like to play billiard and tennis (not considering any of the restrictions): $B = 7$ and $T = 3.5$ (point G^1 in Fig. 10.2). We immediately see that this solution is not feasible. The goal values lie outside the shaded area (see Fig. 10.2). Traditional Goal Programming resolves the problem by minimizing the distance from the goal point (G^1) to the feasible area (shaded area). Which point is the "closest", depends on the distance metric used. We could try the Euclidean distance or Euclidean metric, which is the "ordinary" straight-line distance between two points. (Currently assume that the "closest" solution is nondominated.)

(continued)

Example 10.2 (continued)

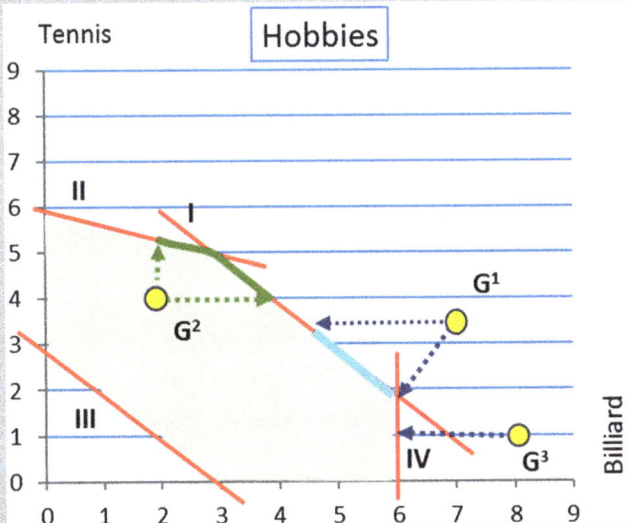

Fig. 10.2 Illustrating the basic idea of goal programming

Consider goal point G^1. The set of good feasible (and nondominated) candidates for the "closest" point lie on the light blue line segment in Fig. 10.2. These points are reasonable in the sense that the goal point G^1 dominates all of them. The nearest good (nondominated) point in the Euclidean sense in this case is $B = 6$ and $T = 2$. Of course, there are other candidates as well.

Note that it is not always possible to find a nondominated (and feasible) solution, which is dominated by a given goal point. An example of such a point is G^3 ($B = 8$ and $T = 1$). G^3 dominates, for example, point $B = 6$ and $T = 1$, which is dominated.

What if James specified a feasible point, such as G^2 as his goal point. The problem is that G^2 is dominated, for instance, by point $B = 3$ and $T = 5$. Normally in Goal Programming such a dominated point is projected onto the nondominated frontier. Again, we use the distance minimization idea between the goal point and the nondominated frontier. It would be logical to consider points which lie on the two green line segments as candidates for the closest point (in Fig. 10.2). They dominate the given goal point G^2.

The main philosophy underlying Goal Programming is to find a solution, which satisfies the decision-maker's needs (or wishes), but which can be put into practice. That is why possible 'optimality' (whatever this means) of the solution is not the most important feature. Pekka Korhonen once discussed the importance of optimality with a well-known Goal Programming expert, Professor James Ignizio. He participated in the Apollo Lunar program as a project manager, and he used that project as an example to illustrate the importance of satisfaction over optimality in decision-making. He said that in his view it was more important to generate a solution which could be implemented rather than a solution, which was 'optimal' (for some version of the problem), but which was not the solution for the actual, real-world problem.

In Goal Programming, it is possible to weigh the deviations from the goals. In this case all the unwanted deviations are multiplied by weights, reflecting their relative importance. Then we would 'minimize' the weighted sum of deviations from the goals.

Goal Programming can also be used in a lexicographic sense. This means that the undesirable deviations from the target are ranked 'lexicographically'. In other words, the highest ranked (most important deviation) is infinitely more important than the second most important deviation, and so forth. Example 10.3 can be used to illustrate this feature.

Example 10.3 Tennis-Billiard Example Revisited
Assume that "some other day" James has the solution $B = 8$ and $T = 1$ (G^1 in Fig. 10.3) in his mind, because that day he is more interested in billiard than tennis. He notices that the solution is not within the constraints he has specified, in other words it is not feasible. Assume James would like to maximize the time he plays billiard, so he maximizes B subject to the constraints. The model allows him to use 6 h for billiard (see point Q^1 in Fig. 10.3). Is there still any time left for tennis? He maximizes the time (T) for tennis, provided the time (B) for billiard is 6 (see point Q^2 in Fig. 10.3). James is happy to find out that it is still possible to play tennis for 2 h.

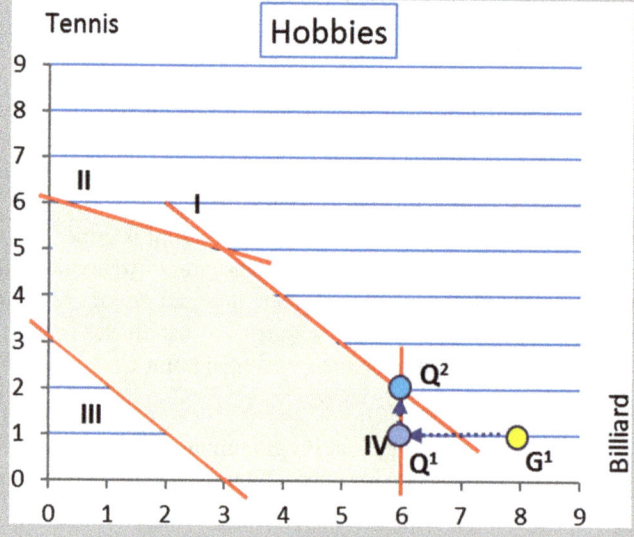

Fig. 10.3 An example of lexicographic goal programming

A major strength of Goal Programming is its simplicity and ease of use. This accounts for the large number of Goal Programming applications in many diverse fields. Linear goal programs can be solved using Linear Programming software as either a single linear program, or in the case of the lexicographic variant, a series of connected linear programs.

Goal Programming can handle relatively large numbers of variables, constraints and objectives. A weakness of Goal Programming is that it may generate solutions which are dominated. However, techniques are available to detect when this occurs and project the solution onto the nondominated frontier.

The specification of appropriate weights (for the deviations in targets) in Goal Programming is another area that has caused debate, with some authors suggesting the use of the Analytic Hierarchy Process or various interactive methods for this purpose.

10.3 Appendix: Illustrating the Decision and Criterion Spaces

The 'design' problem can be represented in terms of the decision variables (the decision variable space or the x-space), or even better in terms of the criteria or objectives (the criterion space or the f-space). The criterion space representation is more helpful, since that representation allows us to easily identify the nondominated solutions. We illustrate with an example, which we have used earlier in classroom. The example is also included in the Wikipedia page (Multiple Criteria Decision Making).

The following two-decision variable, two-objective problem in the decision variable space will help demonstrate some of the key concepts graphically. Mathematically inclined readers may consult Ralph Steuer's book (1986) for additional details on MOLP.

Max $f_1(x) = -x_1 + 2x_2$
Max $f_2(x) = 2x_1 - x_2$

subject to

$x_1 \leq 4$
$x_2 \leq 4$
$x_1 + x_2 \leq 7$
$x_1 - x_2 \leq 3$
$-x_1 + x_2 \leq 3$
$x_1, x_2 \geq$

In the presence of multiple objectives, 'optimizing' each of them separately usually leads to different solutions. Which solution the decision-maker prefers depends on her preferences, that is how she weighs the different objectives.

Fig. 10.4 Demonstration of the decision space

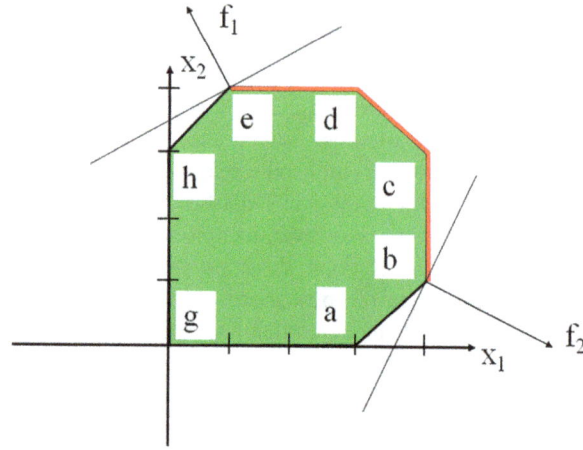

In Fig. 10.4, the extreme points 'e' and 'b' maximize the first and second objectives, respectively. The red boundary between these two extreme points represents the efficient set, although this is not trivial to see from Fig. 10.4. However, for any feasible solution outside the efficient set, it is possible to improve both objectives by moving to points on the efficient set.

Due to its simplicity, the above problem can be represented in criterion (or objective) space by replacing the x's with the f's as follows:[3]

Max f_1
Max f_2

subject to

$f_1 + 2f_2 \leq 12$,
$2f_1 + f_2 \leq 12$,
$f_1 + f_2 \leq 7$,
$f_1 - f_2 \leq 9$,
$-f_1 + f_2 \leq 9$,
$f_1 + 2f_2 \geq 0$,
$2f_1 + f_2 \geq 0$.

We present the criterion (objective) space graphically in Fig. 10.5. It is easier to detect the nondominated points (corresponding to efficient solutions in the decision space) in the criterion space. The north-east region of the feasible space constitutes

---

[3]Note that in more complicated situations it is not possible to explicitly construct the criterion space representation. However, the concepts of efficiency and nondominance generalize to higher dimensions.

Fig. 10.5 Demonstration of the solutions in the criterion space

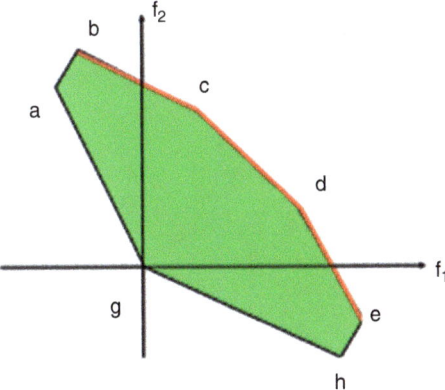

the set of nondominated points for maximization problems (the red piecewise linear curve).

References

Charnes, A., & Cooper, W. W. (1961). *Management models and industrial applications of linear programming*. New York: Wiley.

Charnes, A., Cooper, W. W., & Ferguson, R. (1955). Optimal estimation of executive compensation by linear programming. *Management Science, 1*, 138–151.

Gass, S., & Assad, A. (2005). *An annotated timeline of operations research: An informal history*. New York: Kluwer.

Ignizio, J. P. (1976). *Goal programming and extensions*. Lexington, MA: Lexington Books.

Lee, S. M. (1972). *Goal programming for decision analysis*. Philadelphia: Auerbach.

Steuer, R. E. (1986). *Multiple criteria optimization: Theory, computation, and application*. Chichester: Wiley.

Chapter 11
Solving Design Problems

In the presence of multiple objectives, 'optimizing' each of them separately usually leads to different solutions. Which solution the decision-maker prefers depends on her preferences, that is how she weighs the different objectives.

Throughout our book, the set of nondominated alternatives or solutions (or frontier) has played a key role. This is equally true for 'design' problems. A rational decision-maker would only choose a nondominated solution (alternative). In problems where we can list all decision alternatives, it is a relatively simple task to weed out the dominated alternatives. For 'design' problems, it is not trivial to generate nondominated solutions in general, and good nondominated solutions in particular. This chapter, at a nontechnical level, discusses different ideas how this can be accomplished. We illustrate our ideas with figures. For additional details see Steuer (1986).

11.1 Weighted Sums

We have discussed at some length the use of (importance) weights in Chap. 9 in the context, where all decision alternatives are known. What we wrote in that chapter, is true in the framework of the 'design' problem as well.

Interestingly, already in the mid-1950s, Saaty showed that using (positive) weighted sums of criteria can be used to generate nondominated solutions for convex problems (see Appendix for a definition of a convex set). See the history book by Saul Gass and Arjang Assad for Saaty's contributions.

If you want to focus on finding the most preferred nondominated solution, the critical question becomes, which weights to use and how to elicit them. In fact, the 'problem with the weights' has inspired dozens of researchers to develop their favorite approach to eliciting weights in the 'design' (or mathematical programming) framework. Early research would call them interview techniques, and research starting in early 1970s called them interactive man-machine approaches. In such approaches, phases of computation would alternate with phases of decision-making. Scholars increasingly realized that preferences (the weights) did not necessarily exist, but were something that the decision-maker would learn about or discover while solving the problem. Commonly no explicit knowledge of a multi-attribute value function describing the decision-maker's preferences was assumed, but it was implicitly assumed to have a specific form.

Early work by Zionts and Wallenius was based on operating with weighted sums of objectives (Zionts and Wallenius 1976).

Zionts and Wallenius Algorithm
1. Begin the process by assuming some arbitrary weights. If no other information existed, start with equal weights.
2. Use the current set of weights to generate a nondominated solution. This problem was a Linear Programming problem.
3. Then ask the decision-maker to tell us, whether any of the 'neighboring' solutions were preferred to the current solution. If not, we had found the Most Preferred Solution. If at least one of the neighboring solutions was preferred, we would continue the process. In Appendix B, the formulation is presented to generate new consistent weights. Then return to Step 2, which usually would generate an improved solution.

In the 1970s many corporations were using Linear Programming models to help plan their operations. Our idea was that it would be a relatively easy task to implement our algorithm as part of the planning process. The beauty of our algorithm was that it allowed the use of multiple, conflicting criteria, yet it was built on (at the time) well-known Linear Programming modelling framework.

Let us see how James will solve his problem using the Zionts-Wallenius algorithm.

> **Example 11.1 Tennis-Billiard Example Revisited**
> Because James seemed to be more interested in tennis than billiard, it is natural to start from the maximum value of tennis. Accordingly, let us use as the starting weights for the objectives $w_{tennis} = 1$ and $w_{billiard} = 0$. When James solves the Linear Programming problem by using the objective function: $w_{billiard}B + w_{tennis}T$, he will generate solution Q^1 ($B = 0$ and $T = 6$) in Fig. 11.1. Solution Q^1 is clearly non-dominated.
>
> (continued)

Example 11.1 (continued)

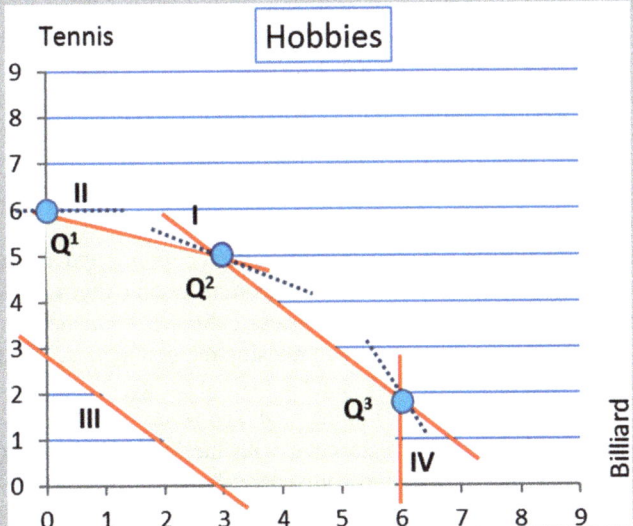

Fig. 11.1 Illustration of the Zionts-Wallenius algorithm

Next, the algorithm asks him to compare all adjacent non-dominated solutions to Q^1. In this simple example, there is only one such solution, namely Q^2. We assume that James prefers Q^2 to Q^1. The approach generates new weights for B and T in such a way that the optimal solution of the new weighted sum cannot any more be Q^1. Assume that the new solution is Q^3. Now the (only) non-dominated adjacent solution to Q^3 is Q^2. Assume James prefers Q^2 to Q^3. Now the weights are updated in such a way that the optimal solution can be neither Q^1 nor Q^3. The final optimal solution is the non-dominated extreme point[1] solution: Q^2.

A critical phase in the Zionts-Wallenius algorithm is the updating of the weights of the objectives. This phase is implemented in such a way that the method will quickly find the most preferred nondominated extreme point solution. To find a non-extreme solution (which lies between extreme point solutions), which would be better than the best extreme point solution, the authors proposed to carry out a local search in the environment of the best extreme point solution.

---

[1] In Linear Programming, the 'corner' solutions (corresponding to intersections of constraints) are called extreme point solutions. An optimal solution of a Linear Programming problem is always an extreme point solution. Hence the significance of the extreme point solutions.

11.2 Reference Point Method

A Polish mathematician, Andrzej Wierzbicki, developed a simple idea to move around (or "jump" from one point to another) on the efficient frontier and published it in 1980. He referred to his idea as the 'Reference Point Method'.

The method is quite similar to Goal Programming, but differs from it in a significant detail. The Reference Point Method projects any given point (goal) onto the nondominated frontier, without making a difference whether the given point is feasible or infeasible. The key idea is to use a projection function which always finds a nondominated solution.

The method is interactive. The DM provides different points and as feedback, the method returns a feasible nondominated point (extreme or no-extreme) "close" to the given goal point. The DM continues the process until she is satisfied or gets tired. The feedback guides the decision-maker in revising the goal points. In other words, she wants something (goal), but does not get it. Instead she gets the solution which is closest (feasible and non-dominated) to the goal, and reacts to it.

Any nondominated point can be reached with the Wierzbicki method. In this sense, it differs from the Zionts-Wallenius-algorithm, which generates so-called nondominated extreme point solutions, until at the end a local search in the environment of the best extreme point is carried out.

We illustrate the use of Wierzbicki's method by Example 11.2. Figure 11.2 is related to this description.

Example 11.2 Tennis-Billiard Example Revisited
Assume that James uses Wierzbicki's method to find his Most Preferred Solution. First, James gives the infeasible ("too optimistic") reference point (goal) G^1 (6.5, 4.0). The approach returns him point Q^1 (5.25, 2.75), which is feasible and nondominated. He realizes that he tried to get too much and reduces the value of B for his goal, and proposes as his new updated reference or goal point G^2 (1.2, 4). The system tells James that the point is unnecessarily pessimistic and returns point Q^2 (2.4, 5.2). This is almost what he wants, but he likes to try once more. Now he uses point G^3 (5, 5) as the reference point. The system returns point Q^3 (4, 4), which he accepts as his Most Preferred Solution. Thus, he spends his day-off playing 4 h tennis and 4 h billiard.

The arrows from reference points G^1, G^2, and G^3 define the direction of projection. The visualization is a simplified presentation of the underlying principles of the method.

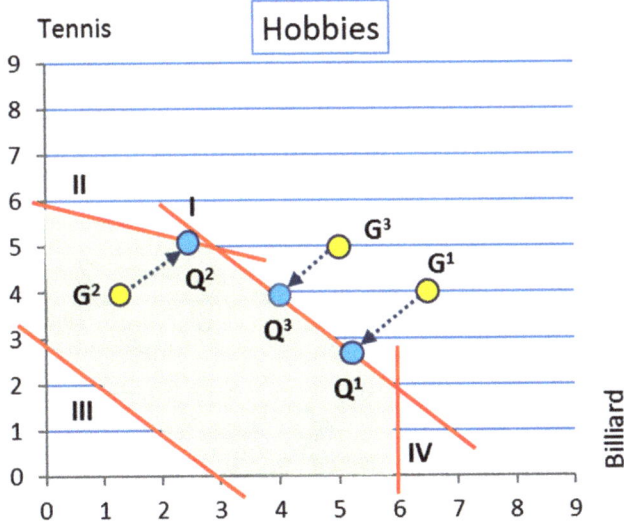

Fig. 11.2 Illustration of the main ideas of the reference point method

11.3 Reference Direction Approach

Korhonen and Laakso extended Wierzbicki's idea in 1986. They proposed that instead of projecting one point at a time onto the non-dominated frontier, an entire given direction is projected. But first we need a starting point (nondominated). The direction is defined as one which starts from the current point and traverses through the given reference (or goal) point. The projection is the path (composed of linear segments), which starts from the current point and continues along the nondominated frontier until we reach the boundary of the frontier.

We revisit the tennis-billiard example.

> **Example 11.3 Tennis-Billiard Example Revisited**
> Assume that James has generated an initial solution Q^0 (2, 5.33) by projecting a reference point onto the frontier. Next, James is asked to tell how he would like to improve the values of his objectives. Let us assume that he defines the reference point G^1 as his new goal. The system generates a direction starting from Q^0, traversing through point G^1, and continuing until the projection reaches the boundary of the nondominated frontier (=the point where the light blue line ends in Fig. 11.3).

(continued)

Example 11.3 (continued)

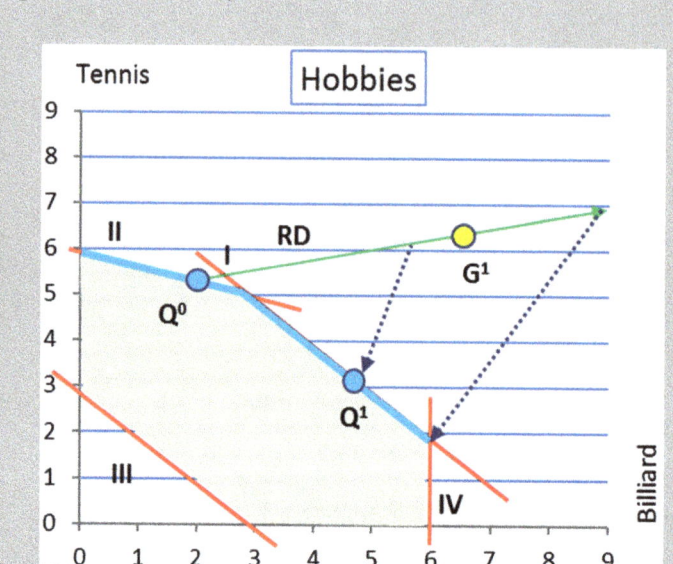

Fig. 11.3 Illustration of the reference direction approach

All values of the objectives (hours of tennis and billiard) are displayed to James on this nondominated path. Next, he is asked to choose the most preferred solution from this path. Let us assume that he chooses Q^1 (4.75, 3.25), is happy with that solution, and ends the process.

The situation can be better illustrated in three dimensions, in which the non-dominated frontier is a rounded surface composed of "mosaic pieces" (parts of planes). Assume that we start the search from a nondominated point Q^0, and specify G^1 as our reference point (goal). The system constructs a line starting from Q^0 and passing through G^1. This green line is projected onto the nondominated frontier (=light blue line in Fig. 11.3). Note that point Q^1 is the projection of G^1.

The values of the objectives on the nondominated frontier can be displayed by using the VIMDA-interface (see Fig. 12.2). The user can freely search the values of the objectives along the nondominated path and choose the solution, which pleases him/her most. Point Q^1 is marked as a special point on the path, since it is the projection of the reference point.

After finding her Most Preferred Solution (from the path), the decision-maker is welcome to provide a new reference point. The new path is defined by means of the new reference direction, which starts from the current solution and goes through the new reference point. The decision-maker should try to find better solutions from the new path. If no better solution is found, the decision-maker is welcome to specify

11.4 Pareto Race

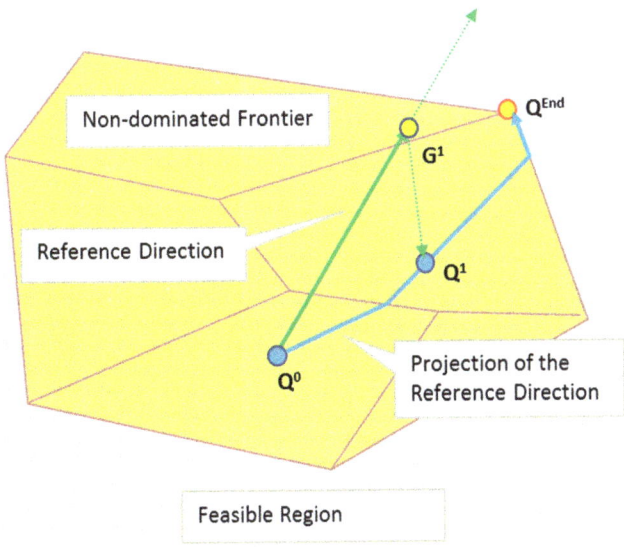

Fig. 11.4 Illustration of the reference direction approach in three dimensions

a new reference direction starting from the currently best solution. If no better solutions can be found, we terminate the process.

Point Q^{end} indicates the end of the non-dominated path. If you end up at Q^{end}, you must do something. You have either to define a new direction, go back or stop your search. The Reference Direction Approach provides you with full freedom to search the nondominated frontier, until you find your Most Preferred Solution. You are not forced to make any choices, which you do not like (Fig. 11.4).

11.4 Pareto Race

Pareto Race was developed by us as a dynamic version of the Reference Direction Approach. In Pareto Race, the user is not required to explicitly determine a reference point for finding a reference direction used to compute a nondominated path (Korhonen and Wallenius 1988).

The user only needs to tell where to start and which objective values to improve and roughly, whether a major or minor improvement is desirable in those objectives. The system, according to instructions from the decision-maker, will automatically turn the reference direction, roughly, according to her wishes. Note that we cannot improve the values of some of the objectives, without at the same time allowing other objectives to get worse. The decision-maker will see the values of the objectives change as we 'travel' along the nondominated frontier. The user can freely search the nondominated frontier (Fig. 11.5).

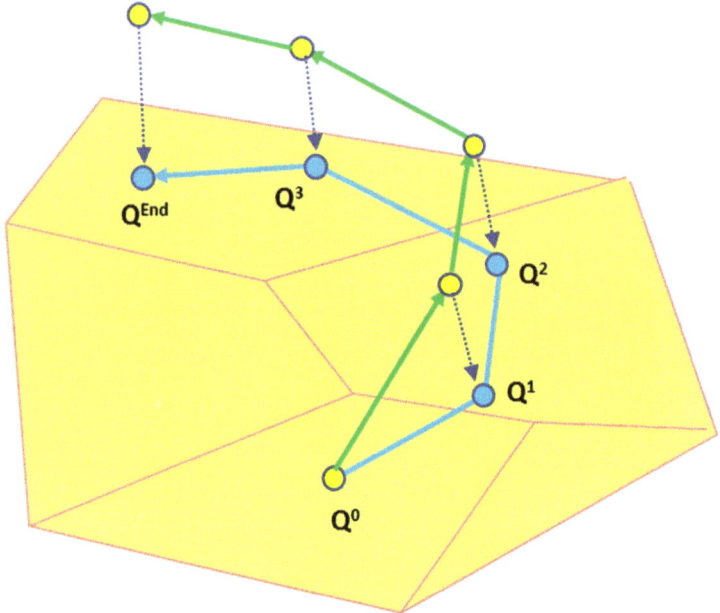

Fig. 11.5 Illustration of Pareto race

When thinking about, how to operationalize the idea of free search (on the nondominated frontier), we decided to simulate driving an automobile. It was, however, far from trivial to figure out how to drive an automobile in, say, a 10-dimensional space (assuming 10 objectives). Brakes (slowing down driving in a specified direction), gears (accelerating), and the gas pedal were easily extended for driving in a 10-dimensional space, but how to steer the car?

A traditional joystick to steer the search works in three dimensions, but a special joystick was needed in 10 dimensions. We solved the problem by using number keys to simulate the moves (left, right, forward, backward) of a joystick. The idea is implemented in the Decision Support System VIG, which we describe in the next chapter.

11.5 A Challenging Nonconvex Feasible Region

Figure 11.6 refers to a mathematically challenging case, where the feasible region is defined with nonlinear restrictions. The first feature, which makes the problem difficult, is the nondominated "frontier". In easy problems, the frontier looks like a frontier, but in hard problems the frontier may be composed of distinct (separate) pieces. In Fig. 11.6, the pieces from A to B, from C to D, and from E to F together form the efficient (nondominated) frontier. Points between B and C are on the exterior of the feasible region; however, they are dominated (by point C).

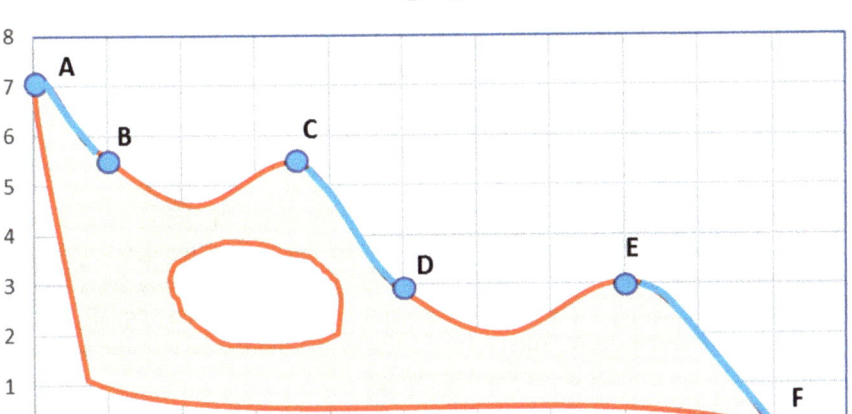

Fig. 11.6 Illustration of a mathematically challenging problem

Another feature, which makes the problem mathematically difficult, is the shape of the feasible set. In easy problems, the set is convex. The feasible set in Fig. 11.6 is not convex. A definition of a convex set implies that when connecting any two points (which belong to the set), the line segment connecting the points is inside the feasible set. If we connect C and E, the line segment is clearly outside the feasible region. Moreover, in a convex set, there are no "holes". The white area in the middle of the feasible region constitutes such a "hole".

In mathematical optimization, one of the reasons, why nonconvex problems are hard to solve, is that if we find a local optimum (best in a certain neighborhood), it is not necessarily the global (overall) optimum.

11.6 Estimating Weights from Pairwise Comparisons

In this model, we assume that the DM's preferences can be represented by a linear value function, in other words using a weighted sum of objectives.

In short, we assume the DM's preferences are represented by a linear value function: $v(X) = \sum_{j=1}^{p} \lambda_j x_j$, where

- p is the number of criteria
- x_j refers to the value of the jth objective
- λ_j refers to the weight of the jth objective (initially unknown)

Assume preferences can be represented by a preference set $P = \{(X_r, X_s) | X_r \succ X_s, r, s \in N\}$. Hence for each pair $(X_r, X_s) \in P$, X_r is the preferred alternative to X_s. Both alternatives are defined according to the aforementioned four criteria $X_r = [x_{r1}, x_{r2}, x_{r3}, x_{r4}]$.

Using the DM's responses, constraints for the Linear Programming weight estimation problem are constructed. For each "I prefer A over B" response, the following inequality restriction is constructed:

$$\sum_{j=1}^{p} \lambda_j x_{Aj} - \epsilon \geq \sum_{j=1}^{p} \lambda_j x_{Bj}$$

A similar constraint is generated conversely, for each "I prefer B over A" response. For the main analysis of results, we will ignore indifference responses. We argue that the answer "I don't know" is ambiguous: we cannot know whether the respondent means that A and B are incomparable, or perhaps exactly equally good, or that she just doesn't know. Therefore, we ignore the indifference responses.

Accordingly, our model to estimate the weights is:

Max ϵ subject to:

$$\sum_{j=1}^{p} \lambda_j x_{rj} - \epsilon \geq \sum_{j=1}^{p} \lambda_j x_{sj}, \text{ for all } (X_r, X_s) \in P$$

$$\sum_{j=1}^{p} \lambda_j = 1$$

$$\lambda_j > 0, \forall j = 1, 2, \ldots, p.$$

In other words, our model seeks to find weights in such a fashion as to maximize the value difference in each pairwise comparison. You will see that this is indeed true, if you move the right-hand term to the left, and move ϵ to the right-hand side. Also note that ϵ over zero means that the DM has answered in a fashion consistent with a linear value function.

References

Korhonen, P., & Laakso, J. (1986). A visual interactive method for solving the multiple criteria problem. *European Journal of Operational Research, 24*, 277–287.

Korhonen, P., & Wallenius, J. (1988). A Pareto race. *Naval Research Logistics, 35*(6), 615–623.

Steuer, R. E. (1986). *Multiple criteria optimization: Theory, computation, and application*. Chichester: Wiley.

Wierzbicki, A. (1980). The use of reference objectives in multiobjective optimization. In G. Fandel & T. Gal (Eds.), *Multiple objective decision making, theory and application*. Heidelberg: Springer.

Zionts, S., & Wallenius, J. (1976). An interactive programming method for solving the multiple criteria problem. *Management Science, 22*, 652–663.

Chapter 12
Need for Decision Support Systems

When facing complex multi-criteria decision problems, there is a need to support decision-makers. In this chapter we outline several computer-based decision support systems, which heavily use computer-graphics. At the time they each represented state-of-the-art technology. We describe the VICO system based on harmonious houses, and the VIMDA system based on line graphs. Both systems support decisions, where we can list all alternatives. The third system, which we describe, is called VIG. It is targeted for supporting decision-making in Multiple Objective Linear Programming environments, where the alternatives are implicitly defined via constraints.

The underlying theory of the VICO system has not been previously described in our book. However, the theory of the VIMDA system (under reference direction approach) and the VIG system (under Pareto Race) have been discussed in the previous chapter. In the current chapter we emphasize the interface and other computer-based decision support aspects of the mentioned approaches.

12.1 Harmonious Houses

In the early 1990s Korhonen developed an approach, which transforms a multi-criteria alternative into a picture in the spirit of Chernoff faces and Andrews curves (Korhonen 1991). However, unlike Chernoff faces (Chernoff 1973) or Andrews curves (Andrews 1972), it also enables a DM to make preference comparisons on the basis of a visual representation. For example, it allows the decision-maker to state, which of two alternatives (represented by a picture) is better.

Korhonen chose to replace the 'face' with a simple 'harmonious house'. The house consists of a roof, walls, one door, and one window. The ideal (standard/normal) house is described in a harmonious (and symmetric) form, where all angles are 90 degree. Deviations from this ideal are perceived abnormal. The degree to which a house resembles the ideal house, serves as the basis for evaluation.

When the value of a criterion or an objective is improving, the icon (the house) becomes "better" looking or more "positive" (harmonious). How the house looks, is controlled by varying the positions of the corner points (of the roof, the door, the window). A criterion is associated with the x- or y-coordinate of any corner point. A deviation from the ideal value is shown as a move in the x- or y-direction. The x- and y-coordinates of corner points are called 'house parameters'. To each corner point, two criteria can be associated, one affecting its horizontal position and the other its vertical position. In total, there are 16 corner points.

An interactive decision support system by name VICO (A VIsual Multiple Criteria COmparison) was developed by Korhonen to implement the above idea. It was targeted for problems with many criteria (not just 2 or 3). VICO would present two alternatives (houses) at a time for the decision-maker's comparison. VICO was tested in two master's theses with 20 student subjects (Kontula 1984; Peiponen 1991). The experimental task consisted of identifying, which three out of 20 companies (hotels) had filed for bankruptcy. The company data consisted of 11 key financial ratios from five consecutive years, such as quick ratio, current ratio, debt- to- equity ratio, sales margin, etc. The subjects compared three approaches:

1. Use of numeric data (that is, no visual aids)
2. Use of Chernoff faces
3. Use of Harmonious houses (VICO)

The tentative results were encouraging from the point of view of the harmonious houses. On average, the subjects chose two bankrupt companies correctly (out of three) using the harmonious houses. This compared favorably against Chernoff faces (1.7 correct choices) and numeric data (1.4 correct choices).

Figure 12.1 refers to the test situation. One of the companies (Yritys 19, on the right) was one of the bankrupt hotels. Note how disharmonious it looks compared to a well-performing company (Yritys 1, on the left). The houses were compared in a pairwise fashion. In other words, the decision-maker was asked to state which of the two houses was preferable (more harmonious).

12.2 VIMDA

A popular approach to visualizing a set of alternatives is to use line graphs. This approach has been used, for example, in Korhonen's VIMDA. VIMDA is essentially a "free search" type of visual, interactive approach for evaluating known alternatives. For the user to benefit from the use of VIMDA, the number of alternatives should be relatively large. In the example below, there are half a million alternatives (Korhonen 1988).

The theoretical basis of VIMDA has been explained in the previous chapter. We recapitulate the main ideas. The system generates a starting alternative. Next the decision-maker gives aspiration levels for the criteria, that is values for the criteria

12.2 VIMDA

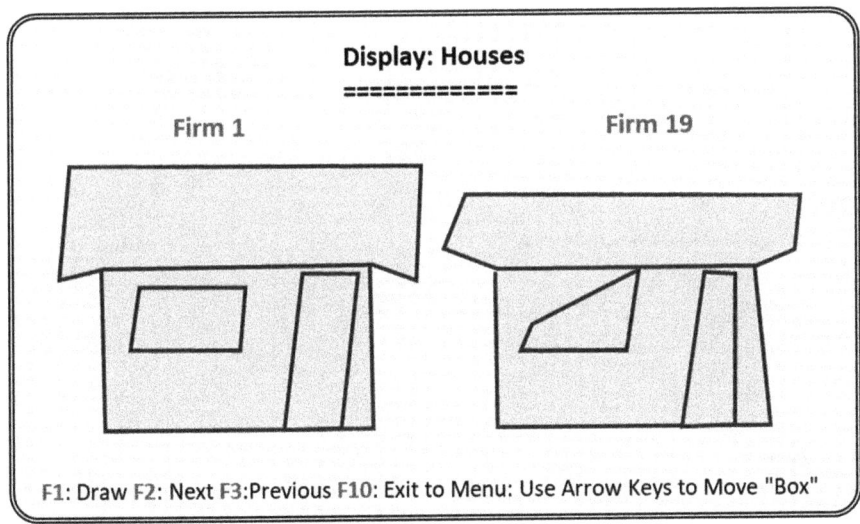

Fig. 12.1 Two harmonious houses: which do you prefer?

the decision-maker would like to achieve. They do not have to be achievable. Normally they are not (with the current resources). Then a direction from the starting (current) solution and passing through the aspiration levels is generated. The closest alternatives to the direction are provided in a graphical form for the decision-maker's evaluation (Fig. 12.2). From this set, she chooses the most preferred alternative, which is used as a new starting alternative for the next iteration. The process continues until the decision-maker is not able to find better alternatives. All alternatives shown are nondominated. The problem is to identify the best alternative from the original set.

The criterion values in Fig. 12.2 are shown on the vertical axis and the alternatives on the horizontal axis. In the table of Fig. 12.2, the best values, the aspiration levels, the worst values, the values of the starting alternative, and the current values of all criteria are displayed. The current alternative is shown in the left-hand margin of the graph.

Each line represents the values of one criterion when we move from one alternative to the next. For instance, criterion 3 (green line) has the best value at the starting alternative; it subsequently decreases throughout. The criterion values of consecutive alternatives have been connected with lines, which stand for the criteria. The cursor characterizes the alternative, whose criterion values are printed numerically at the top of the screen. The alternative "closest" to the values of the aspiration levels is marked with small yellow circles. By moving the cursor, the criterion values are updated. The decision-maker is asked to choose her most preferred alternative from the screen by pointing the cursor to such an alternative.

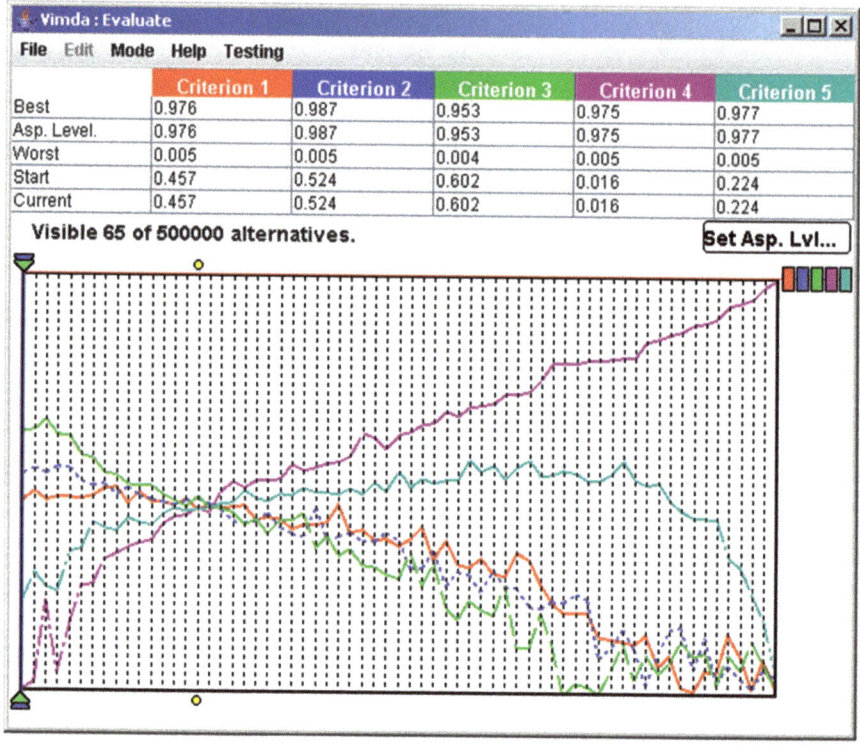

Fig. 12.2 VIMDA's visual interface

12.3 VIG (Pareto Race)

VIG (short for Visual Interactive Goal Programming) is the name of the software, which implements Pareto Race as a dynamic version of the VIMDA approach for design problems (Korhonen 1987). Recall that in design problems the alternatives have been described by a mathematical model. VIG enables decision-makers to move freely on the nondominated frontier and search for their Most Preferred Solution. One cannot violate any behavioral assumptions, because there are none.

Figure 12.3 shows an example of the Pareto Race (or VIG) screen for the Production Planning problem discussed below (Korhonen and Wallenius 1988). In the Production Planning problem, we simultaneously optimize four objectives (two minimized, two maximized). The picture is a snap shop.

In Pareto Race, the decision-maker sees the criterion values change on a display in numeric form and as bar graphs, as she travels along the nondominated frontier. The keyboard controls include an accelerator, gears and brakes. The search on the nondominated frontier is analogous to driving an automobile. The subject can, e.g., increase/decrease speed and brake at any time. It is also possible to change direction, allowing an exploratory search among nondominated solutions.

12.4 Production Planning with VIG (Pareto Race)

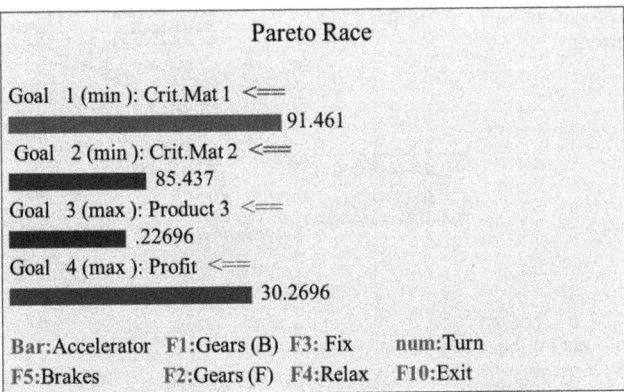

Fig. 12.3 VIG (Pareto race) interface: production planning

The keyboard controls allow the subject to increase/decrease speed at any time. It is also possible (and natural) to change the search direction at any point. As we have explained, this can be accomplished by pressing the (number) key for the objective, whose values we want to improve. For example, if we press number key 1 once, it means that we would like to slightly improve Goal 1 in comparison to other objectives. If we press number key 1 many times, then a more dramatic improvement in Goal 1 takes place (if possible). It is also possible to want to improve more than one objective at a time. In that case, we just press the corresponding number keys, once or several times, depending on the relative desired improvement. If the search direction is not feasible, the decision-maker has to find a new search direction. Note, however, that since we are moving on the nondominated frontier, when some of the objective values improve, some must worsen (by definition).

In one of the early MCDM Conferences, we had a playful contest—who is the fastest Pareto Race driver. The task was to find a given target solution from your starting point as quickly as possible. Colleagues Murat Köksalan and Vahid Lotfi tied for the first place.

For other approaches and associated software systems, the interested reader is asked to consult one of many books on MCDM (Belton and Stewart 2001, or Steuer 1986).

12.4 Production Planning with VIG (Pareto Race)

Next, we will "solve" the Production Planning problem, which we already discussed in Chap. 7. The framework of the problem is described in Fig. 12.4. The objective is to produce three products in such a way that profits are maximized. There are constraining factors, however. The problem sounds straightforward, but in practice there are often complicating features.

Fig. 12.4 The production planning framework

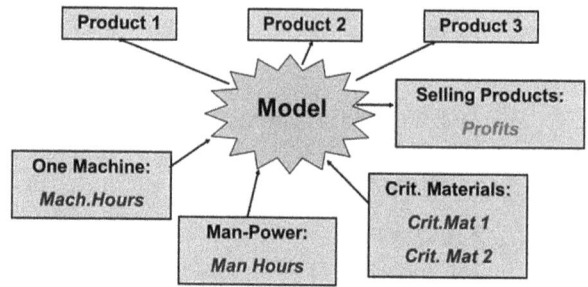

Table 12.1 The data for the production planning problem

	Product 1	Product 2	Product 3		Availability
Machine hours	1.5	1.0	1.6	$\leq$	9
Man hours	1.0	2.0	1.0	$\leq$	10
Critical material 1	9.0	19.5	7.5	$\leq$	96
Critical material 2	7.0	20.0	9.0	$\leq$	96
Profits	4	5	3	$\rightarrow$	Max

Assume that a manager of a small company characterizes her production planning problem as follows:

Example 12.1 Production Planning Problem Revisited
I would naturally like to make as much profit as possible. In the production process we need two Critical Materials. But because they are difficult to get hold of, we would like to primarily avoid ordering more. At this moment, we have 96 units of each. Only one machine is used to produce the products. The machine operates without any problems for at least 9 h, but it is likely to break down if used much more than that. The length of the regular working day is 10 h. One person is needed for this production. She is willing to work overtime, but overtime is costly and she gets tired and is not so efficient the next day. Therefore, I would like to avoid overtime. Finally, Product 3 is very important for a major customer. I cannot totally exclude Product 3 from the production plan.

Assume that all products are measured in the same units. The data are given in Table 12.1. Here is how we read the table. Look, for example, at column 1, corresponding to Product 1. One-unit production (of product 1) consumes 1.5 machine hours, 1 man-hour, 9 units of critical material 1, 7 units of critical material 2, and it will generate 4 units of profits, and so forth. The availability of the resources is also indicated in Table 12.1. The problem is to decide how much to produce each product.

We start with the single-objective Linear Programming problem by maximizing profits subject to all resource constraints. We refer to production amounts of Product

12.4 Production Planning with VIG (Pareto Race)

Table 12.2 The LP-solution for the production planning problem

	Given values	Computed values
Machine hours	9	9.0
Man hours	10	10.0
Critical material 1	96	94.5
Critical material 2	96	88.0
Profits	Max	31.0
Product 1	≥ 0	4
Product 2	≥ 0	3
Product 3	≥ 0	0

Table 12.3 The MOLP-solution for the problem

	Given values	Computed values
Machine hours	9	9.00
Man hours	10	9.73
Critical material 1	Min	91.46
Critical material 2	Min	85.44
Profits	Max	30.27
Product 1	≥ 0	3.88
Product 2	≥ 0	2.81
Product 3	Max	0.23

1, Product 2, and Product 3 by x_1, x_2, and x_3, respectively. We repeat the mathematical problem formulation here:

$$\begin{aligned}
\text{maximize} \quad & 4x_1 + 5x_2 + 3x_3 \\
& 1.5x_1 + x_2 + 1.6x_3 \leq 9 \\
& x_1 + 2x_2 + x_3 \leq 10 \\
& 9x_1 + 19.5x_2 + 7.5x_3 \leq 96 \\
& 7x_1 + 20x_2 + 9x_3 \leq 96 \\
& x_1, x_2, x_3 \geq 0
\end{aligned}$$

The solution of the Linear Programming problem is given in Table 12.2 (Column: Computed Values). To maximize profits, we should produce product $1 = 4$ units, product $2 = 3$ units, and product $3 = 0$ units. Machine Hours and Man Hours are used up to the limits. Neither Critical Materials is fully used. The problem with this solution, however, is that we produce nothing (Product $3 = 0$) for an important client.

Our manager would like to use Multiple Objective Linear Programming (the VIG system) for finding a better solution. An important feature of VIG is that the decision-maker can easily switch the roles of constraints and objectives. Our manager chooses to work with four objectives and two constraints (machine hours, man hours). One important objective is to produce something for an important client (Product 3, max), but simultaneously, she would like to maximize Profits and to minimize the use of Critical Materials.

The values of the most important objectives associated with the Most Preferred Solution are displayed in Table 12.3. In this table Profit is marginally lower than in Table 12.2 but an important client will obtain something, and Critical Materials are used less than before.

12.5 A Digression: How Much Support Is Desirable?

One of our students, Johanna Bragge (née Pajunen) wrote her master's thesis about experimentally testing, how much support decision-makers desire (Pajunen 1989). The thesis was structured around using VIMDA in four different ways, from simple to more complex:

1. Support Level 1: Allows you to scroll all alternatives, delete uninteresting ones, and highlight interesting ones
2. Support Level 2: In addition to support 1, allows you to define acceptable bounds for different attributes (to eliminate alternatives)
3. Support Level 3: In addition to support 1 and 2, allows you to identify and eliminate dominated alternatives
4. Support Level 4: Full-scale VIMDA

The problem was that of buying an apartment (or a condominium) in the Helsinki metro area. The flats were actual homes for sale (at the time). In our experiment, the total number of flats was 98. Their attractiveness was measured with five criteria:

1. Asking price (Finnish marks)
2. Size of the flat (sq. meters)
3. Number of rooms
4. Condition of the flat (rated 1–6; 1 = unit in need of remodeling; 6 = best, corresponding to a new flat)
5. Neighborhood (rated from 1 to 6; 6 refers to best neighborhoods; representative examples were given)

Hence the decision matrix consisted of 5 columns (corresponding to the criteria) and 98 rows (corresponding to the flats).

In total, 78 subjects, who were either 2nd or 3rd year bachelor's students at the Helsinki School of Economics, participated in the experiment. Each of the subjects tested one of the support levels. Hence, roughly, 20 subjects tested each support level.

Pajunen wanted to study a number of questions:

- What was the subject's attitude toward the interface (subjective rating)?
- Did subjects choose dominated alternatives, if the system did not eliminate them?
- Did the subjects behave transitively?[1]

---

[1] Definition of transitivity: if alternative A is preferred to B, and alternative B is preferred to C, then by transitivity A is preferred to C.

- Satisfaction with the most preferred alternative (subjective rating)?
- How long did subjects go on with the search?

We briefly review the main findings. Interestingly, in terms of most performance measures, there were no statistically significant differences. The subjects' subjective perception was that they found quite good solutions with any of the support levels. The search took roughly 20 min, irrespective of the support level.

In terms of dominance, support level 1 was inferior. It led subjects to choose dominated alternatives in one third of the cases. Using support level 2, only 1 subject chose a dominated alternative. Support levels 3 and 4 make sure that all alternatives presented by the system were nondominated.

What can we learn from the previous exercise? Interestingly, most subjects felt confident or fairly confident that their most preferred alternative was nondominated. This was also true for individuals whose most preferred alternative was dominated. It is clear to us that people need help with dominance. Secondly, it is not always true that more support is better than less support. The answer may very well depend on the problem being solved and also the individual. More research is needed to answer the question: how much support is desirable?

References

Andrews, D. (1972). Plots of high dimensional data. *Biometrics, 28*, 125–136.
Belton, V., & Stewart, T. J. (2001). *Multiple criteria decision analysis: An integrated approach*. New York: Kluwer Academic Publishers.
Chernoff, H. (1973). Using faces to represent points in k-dimensional space graphically. *Journal of American Statistical Association, 68*, 361–368.
Kontula, J. (1984). *Moniulotteisen liiketaloudellisen informaation esittäminen graafisesti Chernoffin menetelmällä*. Masters thesis, Helsinki School of Economics.
Korhonen, P. (1987). VIG: A visual interactive support system for multiple criteria decision making. *Belgian Journal of Operations Research, Statistics and Computer Science, 27*, 3–15.
Korhonen, P. (1988). A visual reference direction approach to solving discrete multiple criteria problems. *European Journal of Operational Research, 34*, 152–159.
Korhonen, P. (1991). Using harmonious houses for visual pairwise comparison of multiple criteria alternatives. *Decision Support Systems, 7*, 47–54.
Korhonen, P., & Wallenius, J. (1988). A Pareto race. *Naval Research Logistics, 35*, 615–623.
Pajunen, J. (1989). *Eriasteisen tuen merkitys päätöksentekijän valintakäyttäytymiselle monitavoitteisessa päätöksenteossa*. Masters thesis, Helsinki School of Economics.
Peiponen, P. (1991). *Monitavoitteisten päätösvaihtoehtojen visuaalinen paremmuusvertailu*. Masters thesis, Helsinki School of Economics.
Steuer, R. (1986). *Multiple criteria optimization: Theory, computation, and application*. New York: Wiley.

Chapter 13
Use Scenarios Instead of a Crystal Ball

Using crystal balls for fortune telling and clairvoyance was common in the Roman Empire and in the middle ages. This started changing in mid-1600s, when Pascal and Fermat started to collaborate. Their purpose was to develop a method to predict mathematical futures. In a series of letters to each other, Pascal and Fermat laid the foundation for modern probability (Devlin 2008). To deal with uncertainty (or risk), decision analysts have normally resorted to probabilities.

The problem with probabilities in decision-making is that we seldom have access to objective probabilities. Instead of objective probabilities, we frequently have to resort to subjective probabilities. Subjective probability is a probability derived from an individual's personal judgment or own experience about whether a specific outcome is likely to occur. It only reflects the person's subjective opinion and past experience about the likelihood of an event. There is ample literature emphasizing the difficulty of subjective probability assessment. One of the better-known articles is Hogarth (1975).

In this chapter, we introduce Scenario Analysis (Hassani 2016; Spaniol and Rowland 2019). Many, who work with scenarios, use probabilities. The probabilities in Scenario Analysis do not, however, have to be exact. Often, they have been specified in a "fuzzy", or nonquantitative way. In this chapter, we initially estimate and operate with probabilities. Then we show, how we can work with scenarios without probabilities. In that case, in the spirit of MCDM, different scenarios are treated as objectives.

Crystal Ball is also a well-known software product for risk analysis. Obviously, we do not mean this software.

13.1 What Is Scenario Analysis?

According to Wikipedia:

"Scenario Analysis is a process of analyzing future events by considering alternative possible outcomes (sometimes referred to as "alternative worlds"). Thus, Scenario Analysis, which is one of the main forms of projection, does not try to show one exact picture of the future. Instead, scenarios present several alternative future developments. Consequently, a scope of possible future outcomes is observable. Not only are the outcomes observable, also the development paths leading to the outcomes. In contrast to prognoses, the Scenario Analysis is not based on extrapolation of the past. It does not rely on historical data and does not expect past observations to remain valid in the future. Instead, it tries to consider possible developments and turning points ... In short, several scenarios are fleshed out in a Scenario Analysis to show possible future outcomes."

Each scenario normally combines optimistic, pessimistic, and neutral developments. However, all scenarios should be plausible. Experience suggests that using around three scenarios is most appropriate for further analysis. If we incorporate more than three scenarios, the analysis may get overly complicated. In Scenario Analysis, one of the scenarios (basic scenario or expected scenario) often receives most consideration.

For instance, if we consider various investment strategies, we are definitely interested in the development of the economy. Even if we cannot exactly know, how the national or global economy will develop, we have a hunch what happens, for instance, in the worst or best case. We may also be able to evaluate, how possible or likely the various scenarios are. This way, we will have a better chance to plan our actions to meet the uncertain future. The interested reader may consult Vilkkumaa et al. (2018) or Bradfield et al. (2005) for additional details.

Let us consider a simple example to illustrate Scenario Analysis.

Example 13.1 Where to Spend Holidays

Suppose that the family dinner table conversation focuses on, where to spend the summer holidays. The family has two basic options in mind: to spend holidays in the home country (Finland) or go abroad (warm country). If the forthcoming summer is nice and warm at home, it is not a bad option to spend holidays in the home country. On the other hand, no one is willing to spend the holidays in rainy and cold weather.

You may approach the problem by specifying the following possible weather scenarios (for the summer), which characterize the weather circumstances accurately enough:

(a) Cold and rainy
(b) Warm and rainy

(continued)

Example 13.1 (continued)
(c) Cold and dry
(d) Warm and dry

Next, the family members have to decide how to evaluate the two decisions. Let us assume that they focus just on two criteria:

1. Happiness of the family members
2. Price (cost) of the holiday

Suppose the family estimates probabilities for the different weather scenarios, and formulates the choice problem as follows:

Now the family has the relevant information available. The problem is, how to use it? First, the family may consider, which scenario is most probable in each decision. In the "Stay home" option, the most probable scenario (0.4) is "Warm and Rainy". It makes the family unhappy, but the option is cheap. Correspondingly, the most probable scenario (0.7) is "Warm and Dry" for the "Go abroad" option. This option makes the family members happy, but it is costly.

Let us simplify the problem a bit. The scenarios "Cold and Rainy" and "Cold and Dry" are clearly the worst-case scenarios associated with the "Stay home" option. The "Warm and Rainy" scenario is not good, if you decide to "Go abroad". Thus, remaining scenarios are "Warm and Dry" related to both decisions and "Warm and Rainy" related to "Stay home". Thus, the probability is 0.7 that the worst-case scenarios do not become true. If we ignore the worst-case scenarios, we basically only need to compare the Happy & Costly consequences of the "Go abroad" option against the Unhappy or Happy & Cheap consequences of the "Stay home" option. After simplifying the problem in this way, the choice boils down to the question, how big of a holiday budget the family is planning to spend. "Going abroad" will give the family a better chance of being able to enjoy nice weather, if they can afford it (Fig. 13.1).

13.2 Using Scenario Analysis for Financial Institutions

13.2.1 Capital and Analysis Review by the Federal Reserve[1]

A common form of Scenario Analysis, often required by regulators, is to test the resilience of financial and other institutions against possible future crises. We call it stress testing. Stress testing is often carried out using computer simulation.

---

[1]This section is based on Federal Reserve's publicly posted information regarding Comprehensive Capital and Analysis Review.

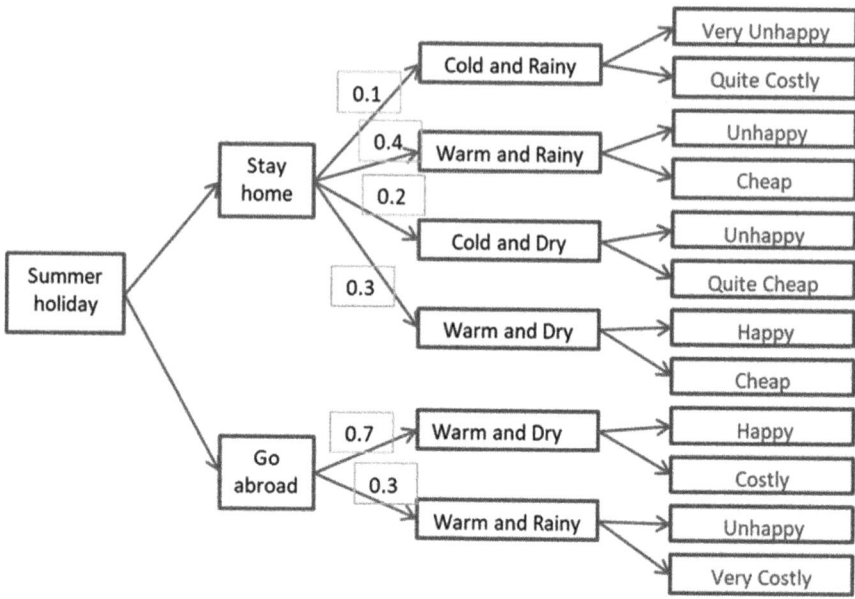

Fig. 13.1 Summer holiday choice problem

The Federal Reserve conducts the annual Comprehensive Capital and Analysis Review (CCAR) exercise to assess capital positions and to make sure that planning practices of large firms are consistent with U.S. regulations. The Federal Reserve conducts a quantitative assessment of firms' capital positions in CCAR using the Dodd-Frank Act stress tests (DFAST). In the financial sector, stress tests make sure that banks have adequate capital to guard themselves against possible losses. They also make sure that banks will be able to lend to households and businesses even in times of severe recessions. The Dodd-Frank Act stress tests also help ensure that banks can continue to lend during times of stress. Both tests only apply to domestic (that is, U.S.) bank holding companies and foreign bank intermediate holding companies with more than $100 billion in total consolidated assets.

The stress tests use three hypothetical scenarios: baseline, adverse, and severely adverse. For 2019, the severely adverse scenario features a severe global recession in which the U.S. unemployment rate would rise to 10%. The severely adverse scenario also includes higher risks for corporate loan and commercial real estate markets.

The adverse scenario features a moderate recession in the United States, as well as weakening economic activity abroad.

The adverse and severely adverse scenarios describe hypothetical events designed to test the strength of banks and large firms. The baseline scenario is in line with average projections from economic forecasters. It does not represent the forecast of the Federal Reserve. Each scenario includes 28 variables, such as Gross Domestic Product, the unemployment rate, stock market prices, and interest rates, covering domestic and international economic activity. The Board also publishes a verbal description of the scenarios, highlighting changes from last year.

Firms who are engaged in large-scale trading are required to factor in a global market shock component as part of their scenarios.

13.2.2 Other Applications

Financial institutions commonly use Scenario Analysis to deal with several possible scenarios for the economy (e.g. rapid growth, moderate growth, slow growth) and for financial market returns (for bonds, stocks and cash) in each of those scenarios. A traditional way is to estimate the probabilities for different scenarios. To help decision-making, the scenario-weighted expected return can also be calculated.

Other interesting examples of application areas are competition analysis, strategic planning, and launching a new product.

Furthermore, businesses can use Scenario Analysis to analyze the potential financial outcomes of certain decisions, such as selecting one of two facilities or stores from which the business could operate.

Simulation is the most common tool for Scenario Analysis. For instance, in a stress test, an action is specified using the values for the relevant variables, and then after certain computations the system gives an answer. By varying the starting values, we learn which kind of combinations lead to a favorable result or help us avoid worst-case solutions. This means the analysis is performed in the "what—if" spirit.

13.3 Multiple Criteria Decision Making with Scenarios

There are many problems which we may approach in the "What to do—to achieve" spirit. We will next show, how to approach the investment problem by combining Scenario Analysis with MCDM.

> **Example 13.2 Investing Your Mother-In-Law's Money**
> Assume that you are managing a portfolio for your 70-year old conservative mother-in-law. The mother-in-law is not poor, though not wealthy. The mother-in-law currently has €100,000 to invest. We have identified four possible investments for the next calendar year. The returns are known for certain, should given states of the economy hold. We assume three states for the economy: declining, stable, and improving. To begin with, we assume that
>
> (continued)

> **Example 13.2** (continued)
> we know the probabilities of the different states. Exactly one of the states will occur.
> The investments are as follows:
>
> - Bond Fund (Fund 1)—This fund is conservative and gives a low return if the economy is stable or improves, and loses a small amount if the economy declines.
> - Money Market Fund (Fund 2)—This fund is very conservative, and never loses money. It gives a small return regardless of the state of the economy.
> - Aggressive Stock Fund (Fund 3)—This fund is aggressive, and does very well if the economy is stable or improves, but loses substantially if the economy declines.
> - Contrarian Fund (Fund 4)—This fund is aggressive, but contrarian, and does very well if the economy declines. It performs modestly in a stable economy, but loses substantially if the economy improves.

Let us first consider the situation, where you invest only in one fund. In the spirit of Scenario Analysis, we compute the Expected Monetary Value for each fund using the estimated probabilities. We obtain the following values: Fund 1: 2.8%, Fund 2: 2.0%, Fund 3: 6.2%, and Fund 4: 1.4%. Thus, based on the expected values, we invest all €100,000 in Fund 3. This, on the surface, appears fine, but how to cope with the situation when the economy will decline. In that case, you will lose 7%. The Expected Monetary Value does not provide you with that information. Moreover, it assumes the investor to be risk-neutral (Fig. 13.2).

Next, let us approach the investment problem as an MCDM problem (evaluation problem), where we must choose one alternative (and not a portfolio). Accordingly, our problem consists of four known alternatives and three criteria (the return in each state of the economy). Actually, we have four criteria, if we use the expected return as one criterion.

None of the alternatives is dominated. Thus, to invest in any of the four funds is reasonable. The most probable scenarios are "Stable" and "Improving". In light of this information, Fund 3 seems quite attractive. However, if the economy declines, the loss is big. By choosing Fund 1, we probably make some money, without losing much in the worst-case scenario. If you are reluctant to the idea of losing at all, Fund 2 would be a good choice for you.

Now let us follow Markowitz's idea of diversifying your portfolio, and allow investing in several funds at the same time. Accordingly, let us formulate the problem as a design problem (Multiple Objective Linear Programming). To search for the Most Preferred Solution, we can use the Pareto Race-interface, which is included in the VIG-software. The purpose is to find the most preferred allocation between the funds by maximizing the return for each state of the economy. Because

13.3 Multiple Criteria Decision Making with Scenarios

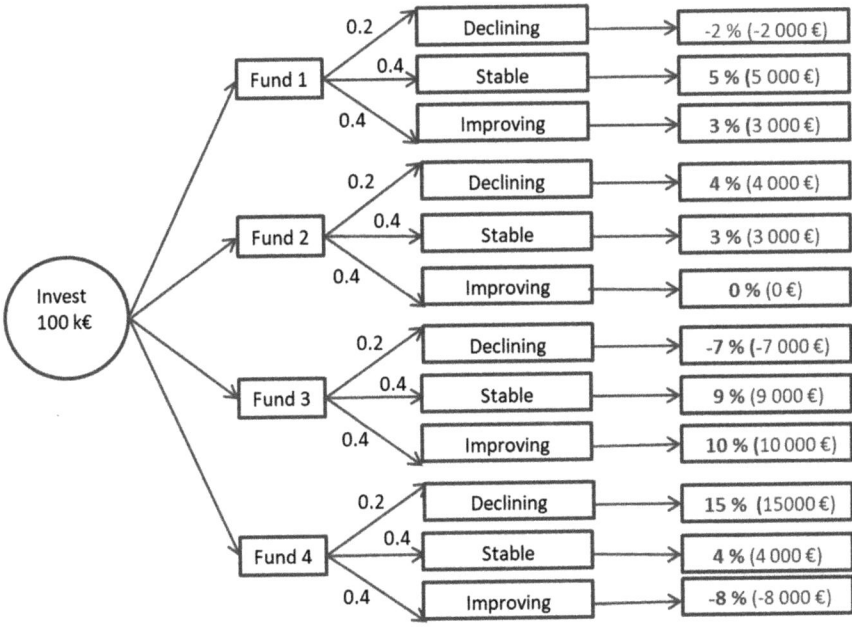

Fig. 13.2 Investing €100,000 under uncertain economy

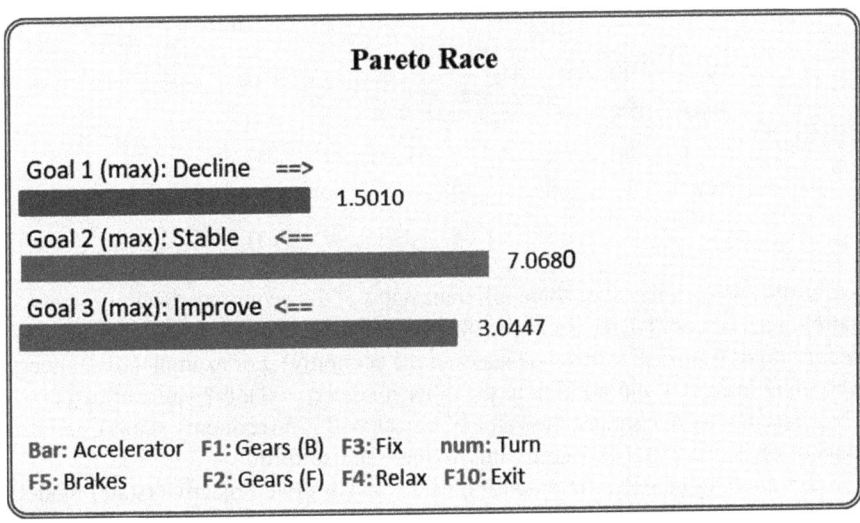

Fig. 13.3 Pareto race screen: potential most preferred solution

there is no uniquely best solution for the problem, Pareto Race helps the DM search the nondominated frontier, until she is happy with the solution.

In Fig. 13.3, we have displayed a potentially Most Preferred Solution. In this solution, the returns are 1.5% if the economy declines, 7.1% if it stays stable, and

3.0% if it improves. The underlying allocation (which you cannot see on the screen) consists of investing 61.36% in Fund 3 and 38.64% in Fund 4 (of the 100,000 euros).

Note that the Pareto Race solution ignored the explicit probabilities for the different states of the economy. Instead, in the MCDM spirit, when searching for the Most Preferred Solution, we implicitly paid attention to the likelihoods of the different states of the economy (in our head). If we think that the declining economy deserves more weight, we act accordingly. The solution generated is balanced. Even if things turn bad, we avoid incurring losses. For the case of a stable economy, the outcome is excellent; for the improving economy, the outcome is not great, but not bad either. If you want to, we can easily calculate the expected return using the estimated probabilities for the Pareto Race investment: 4.35%.

It is also possible to use the expected return as the fourth objective, if we have faith in the probability assessments. Two model versions, without and with the expected return, are presented in the Appendix.

13.4 Appendix: A MOLP Formulation for Investment Planning

Our model is a Multiple Objective Linear Programming model, which can be used to find the most preferred allocation of Funds x_i ($i = 1, 2, 3, 4$). We can diversify our portfolio; hence we can invest in several (or all) of the funds.

$$
\begin{aligned}
max \quad & -2x_1 + 4x_2 - 7x_3 + 15x_4 \\
max \quad & 5x_1 + 3x_2 + 9x_3 + 4x_4 \\
max \quad & 3x_1 + 10x_3 + 8x_4 \\
s.t. \quad & x_1 + x_2 + x_3 + x_4 = 1 \\
& x_1, x_2, x_3, x_4 \geq 0
\end{aligned}
$$

The objectives refer to the three different states of the economy: declining, stable, improving. The coefficients for each column refer to the case of investing in each of the four funds (returns for different states of the economy). For example, if we invest everything in fund 1 and nothing in the other funds ($x_1 = 1$), the value of objective 1 is -2 (economy declining), the value of objective 2 is 5 (economy stable), and the value of objective 3 is 3 (economy improving), and so forth.

The following model is an extension of the above three-objective (state) model. The coefficients of the fourth objective correspond to the expected returns of the funds. The coefficients are calculated as follows:

$$2.8 \; (= 0.2 \cdot (-2) + 0.4 \cdot 5 + 0.4 \cdot 3),$$

$$2 \,(= 0.2 \cdot 4 + 0.4 \cdot 3),$$
$$6.2 \,(= 0.2 \cdot (-7) + 0.4 \cdot 9 + 0.4 \cdot 10), \text{ and}$$
$$1.4 \,(= 0.2 \cdot (15) + 0.4 \cdot 4 + 0.4 \cdot 8),$$

where 0.2, 0.4, and 0.4 correspond to the probabilities of each scenario: Declining, Stable, and Improving. The assumption with the fourth objective is that we have faith in the estimated probabilities.

$$\begin{aligned}
\max \quad & -2x_1 + 4x_2 - 7x_3 + 15x_4 \\
\max \quad & 5x_1 + 3x_2 + 9x_3 + 4x_4 \\
\max \quad & 3x_1 + 10x_3 + 8x_4 \\
\max \quad & 2.8x_1 + 2x_2 + 6.2x_3 + 1.4x_4 \\
\text{s.t.} \quad & x_1 + x_2 + x_3 + x_4 = 1 \\
& x_1, x_2, x_3, x_4 \geq 0
\end{aligned}$$

References

Bradfield, R., Wright, G., Burt, G., Cairns, G., & van der Heijden, K. (2005). The origins and evolution of scenario techniques in long range business planning. *Futures, 37*(8), 795–812.

Devlin, K. (2008). *The unfinished game*. New York: Perseus Books Group.

Hassani, B. (2016). *Scenario analysis in risk management*. Cham: Springer.

Hogarth, R. (1975). Cognitive processes and the assessment of subjective probabilities. *Journal of the American Statistical Association, 70*, 271–294.

Spaniol, M. J., & Rowland, N. J. (2019). Defining scenario. *Futures & Foresight Science, 1*, e3. https://doi.org/10.1002/ffo2.3.

Vilkkumaa, E., Liesiö, J., Salo, A., & Ilmola-Sheppard, L. (2018). Scenario-based portfolio model for building robust and proactive strategies. *European Journal of Operational Research, 266*(1), 205–220.

Chapter 14
Making Operations More Efficient

To improve performance is one of the key tasks of managers in organizations. Demands to make operations more profitable and efficient is common. Performance is often simply measured with a monetary yardstick: the private-sector firm making most money or the public sector organization operating with the least expenditure is considered to be best.

However, monetary measures do not always capture all aspects of performance. In particular, in the public sector it may be practically—or politically—impossible to attach prices to some goods or services produced: what is the price of a university degree, or of a medical operation saving a human life? We may be able to figure out the short-term costs of some operations, but what is—for instance—the price of a lost opportunity? How expensive it is not to educate, or to lose a life? Thus, performance is clearly multidimensional by nature, and several indicators (outputs) are required to characterize all essential aspects of performance. The factors (inputs) affecting performance are multidimensional as well. In practice, the relationship between outputs and inputs is often complex or unknown, making direct performance evaluation a complicated task.

A key concept in efficiency measurement is productivity, which is defined as the ratio of the output(s) produced to the input(s) used: $\frac{output(s)}{input(s)}$. If we have more than one input/output, then both the inputs and outputs have to be aggregated into a single index by expanding the definition of productivity to a ratio of the weighted sum of outputs and the weighted sum of inputs:

$$Productivity = \frac{\mu_1 Output_1 + \mu_2 Output_2 + \ldots \mu_s Output_s}{\nu_1 Input_1 + \nu_2 Input_2 + \ldots \nu_m Input_m},$$

where s is the number of outputs and m the number of inputs.

Sometimes the weighted sums are called *virtual outputs* and *virtual inputs*. How to select the weights? Traditionally evaluating DMUs with multiple inputs and/or outputs has required information on the prices. DEA offers one possibility to come up with a single aggregated index without the need of having a priori price information.

It is important to make a clear distinction between productivity and efficiency. Productivity is an absolute measure of performance and efficiency relative. The following example describes the differences of those two concepts.

> **Example 14.1 Productivity Versus Efficiency**
> Assume that you go pick blueberries with your two friends. You will spend 4 hours in a forest. You pick 8 liters. Your friend John picks 16 liters and Bill only 4. Your productivity is 2 (=8/4), John's 4 (=16/4), and Bill's 1 (=4/4). Hence, productivity is an absolute measure for output(s)/input(s). When we evaluate efficiency, we compare productivity to the best value. Because John is the best blueberry picker, your efficiency score is 0.5 (=2/4). John's efficiency score is 1 (=4/4), and Bill's only 0.25 (=1/4).

In our book, we focus on relative efficiency.

14.1 Data Envelopment Analysis

A popular approach to performance evaluation is Data Envelopment Analysis (DEA) developed by Charnes, Cooper and Rhodes in late 1970's (Charnes et al. 1978, 1979). Performance evaluation is carried out by comparing Decision Making Units (DMUs) against each other. It is important that the units essentially perform the same task. Examples of such units are schools, fire departments, hospitals, universities, supermarkets, etc. Note that it is not meaningful to compare the performance (or efficiency) of supermarkets and fire departments. In DEA we study, whether it is possible to find another (comparable) unit that produces more outputs with the same usage of inputs, or achieves the same level of output production with less inputs? If such a unit exists, it is quite clear that—other things being equal—the evaluated unit does not operate as well as it could.

In DEA, there is no need to explicitly know the relationship between inputs and outputs. The values of inputs and outputs of the units is the only requisite information for the analysis.

DEA recognizes the units, which should improve their performance and the units which cannot be recognized as poor-performers. DEA identifies technically efficient units, but it is value-free in the sense that it does not consider the importance of various factors (outputs or inputs). In addition to the identification of technically efficient units, DEA provides a score for inefficient units. Efficient units have an efficiency score equal to 1, and inefficient units a score between 0 and 1, but less than 1. The closer the efficiency score is to 1, the more efficient (relatively) the unit is. In many practical applications, the use of importance (or preference) information is necessary.

Most people inevitably associate efficiency with layoffs in the private sector and budget cuts in the public sector. The concept of efficiency itself is rather innocent: it just points out, whether it is possible to develop the firm or the public organization (Decision Making Unit or DMU for short), in such a way that it performs better with the current resources or to maintain the current performance with less resources.

This chapter introduces the main principles of DEA, and how to incorporate preference information in the analysis. There is much in common with DEA and MCDM.

14.2 How to Measure Efficiency?

An essential feature in the efficiency analysis is to provide information how to become efficient. There are two basic principles: you have to produce the same output with less resources or to increase your output with the current resources. In principle, you can simultaneously increase output(s) and decrease input(s). However, this—so-called combined—way is not very common in the efficiency analysis.

When the number of inputs or outputs or both are more than one, then a new feature enters the analysis: How to find the weights for the different inputs and/or outputs? DEA finds weights such that each unit appears in the best light. We demonstrate the underlying principle using the following data set:

Example 14.2 Efficiency of Hypermarkets
In Table 14.1, we have chosen a sample from the population of 25 hypermarkets (in Finland).[1] For the original hypermarkets, we carried out technical and Value[2] Efficiency Analysis. In the original data set, the number of inputs and outputs was six in total, but for our purposes we simplify the situation and just use two outputs (Sales and Profits) and two inputs (The Number of Employees, and the Size of the Market (Floor Space)).

Table 14.1 A sample from the set of 25 hypermarkets

Outputs/inputs	A	B	C	D
Sales (10^6 €)	35.2	13.29	11.5	16.65
Profits (10^6 €)	0.84	0.3	0.25	0.32
Man hours (10^3 h)	150	60	48	69
Floor space (10^3 m^2)	6.3	3.8	2.3	3

---

[1] We have also modified the output and input values.
[2] Value Efficiency is a method developed by us with colleagues, which also considers preference information. We will describe the method later in this chapter.

Let us evaluate the efficiency of unit B. We want to find for unit B the best output/input—ratio (operating with the weights), when all ratios are forced smaller than one. In other words, the maximal productivity is by definition one. If the ratio under consideration is also one, then the unit is efficient. Otherwise, it is inefficient. In other words, DEA finds weights for each unit, which make it look most favorable.

$$max \quad \frac{13.29\mu_1 + 0.3\mu_2}{60\nu_1 + 3.8\nu_2}$$

subject to

$$\frac{13.29\mu_1 + 0.3\mu_2}{60\nu_1 + 3.8\nu_2} \leq 1$$

$$\frac{35.2\mu_1 + 0.84\mu_2}{150\nu_1 + 6.3\nu_2} \leq 1$$

$$\frac{11.5\mu_1 + 0.25\mu_2}{48\nu_1 + 2.3\nu_2} \leq 1$$

$$\frac{16.65\mu_1 + 0.32\mu_2}{69\nu_1 + 3\nu_2} \leq 1$$

$$\mu_1, \mu_2, \nu_1, \nu_2 \geq 0.$$

The problem above is formulated as a Linear Programming model, which makes it easy to solve.[3] As a solution, we get the following information:

- Efficiency score for each unit under consideration. Here the efficiency score for unit B = 0.932 (= the maximum for the above problem). We may also use the expression that "the efficiency of unit B is 93.2%"
- The best possible μ and ν coefficients, i.e. the values which maximize the ratio:

$$\frac{13.29\mu_1 + 0.3\mu_2}{60\nu_1 + 3.8\nu_2}$$

are $\mu_1 = 0.054$, $\mu_2 = 0.686$, $\nu_1 = 0.017$, and $\nu_2 = 0$.[4]

---

[3] Linear Programming models can be solved with Excel Solver.
[4] Units A, C, and D are efficient.

14.2 How to Measure Efficiency?

Table 14.2 A numerical data set for illustration purposes

	A	B	C	D	E	F	G
Output 1	1	2	3	4	4	5	6
Output 2	5	7	4	3	6	5	2

Table 14.3 Efficiency scores and reference units for data set in Table 14.2

Units:	A	B	C	D	E	F	G
Output 1	1	2	3	4	4	5	6
Output 2	5	7	4	3	6	5	2
Ref. units	A	B	C	D	E	F	G
B	1	1					
E			0.71		1		
F			0.29	0.67		1	
G				0.33			1
Eff. scores	0.714	1.000	0.700	0.750	1.000	1.000	1.000

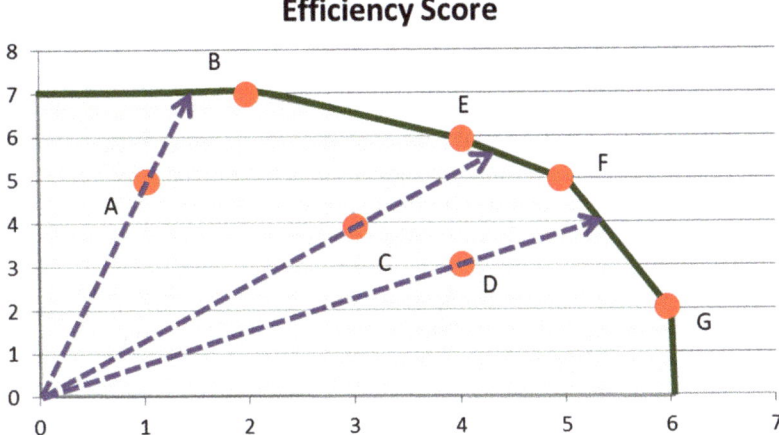

Fig. 14.1 Illustration of efficiency scores and reference units

The efficiency concept in DEA is the same as was introduced in the context of Multiple Objective Linear Programming. Instead of the word "efficient", we use "nondominance" in MOLP.

DEA can also be used to find so called "reference units" (or benchmarks) for inefficient units. We illustrate finding benchmarks using the following numerical data set (Table 14.2), which consists of two outputs and one identical input (value 1 for all units).)

In Table 14.3, the efficiency scores and reference units are given in numerical form and visualized in Fig. 14.1.

Units B, E, F and G are efficient. Their efficiency score is 1, as shown on the last row in Table 14.3. In Fig. 14.1, the efficient units are located on the frontier of the production possibility set, which is the set of possible solutions. The production possibility set is the shaded (light green) area in Fig. 14.1. The dark green piecewise linear curve stands for the efficient frontier.[5]

The dotted lines in Fig. 14.1 describe the so-called 'radial'[6] projections of inefficient units (to the efficient frontier). The efficiency score is measured as the ratio of the length of the vector from the origin to the unit to the total length of the projection (origin to the efficient frontier).[7] From Fig. 14.1, we can see that units A, C, and D are inefficient. Their efficiency scores are 0.714, 0.700, and 0.750, respectively.

The reference units are benchmarking (or model) units for inefficient units. Those units specify the point at which the radial projection meets the efficient frontier. From Fig. 14.1, we see that the projections associated with point C meet the efficient frontier on the line segment between E and F. Respectively, the projection associated with D meets the frontier on the line segment between F and G. Note that there are no points on the frontier, which exactly specify the end point of the projection associated with point A. However, point B dominates the projection point, which is located on the weakly efficient frontier.

The units E and F for unit C, F and G for D, and B for A are called reference units. They are interesting from the point of view of the DM. If the coefficient of a reference unit is big, it tells the DM the unit might be a good existing example unit for an inefficient unit. Of course, the point at which the radial projection ends on the frontier might be better, but it is a virtual, not an existing unit. For instance, for unit C unit E (coefficient $= 0.71$) is, perhaps, a better benchmark example than F (coefficient $= 0.29$).

For readers who are interested in learning more about Data Envelopment Analysis, we recommend the book by Cooper et al. (2007) and the survey article by Emrouznejad and Yang (2018).

14.3 Value Efficiency

Data Envelopment Analysis produces a lot of useful information about similar units, for which the analysis is carried out, for example:

- The best possible (or most favorable) coefficients (weights) for the inputs and outputs of each unit. The coefficients make each unit as efficient as possible.

---

[5] Actually, the line left from unit B and down from unit G stands for the weakly efficient frontier.
[6] The term 'radial' comes from the word 'ray'. The projection is radial, if it linearly continues in the same direction as a ray.
[7] This is an alternative way to illustrate an efficiency score.

14.3 Value Efficiency

- The degree of efficiency of each unit (Efficiency Score), which measures on scale from 0 to 1 (or 0% to 100%), how efficient the unit is. All units can be efficient. However, all units cannot be inefficient, because the comparison is always relative. There is always at least one efficient unit.
- The benchmarks for inefficient units. Such benchmarks are efficient.

The original DEA is value-free in the sense that efficiency evaluation is based on available data without considering the decision-maker's preferences. All efficient DMUs are considered equally "good". However, if the efficient units are not equally preferred by the DM, it is necessary to somehow incorporate the DM's judgments or preferences into the analysis.

We have extensively researched this problem. Our approach is to explicitly or implicitly gather direct preference information about the desirable input- and output-values of DMUs, and insert that information in one form or another into the analysis. We have borrowed some ideas from Multiple Criteria Decision Making (MCDM) research.

In MCDM, one of the key issues is to provide a DM with a tool, which makes it possible to evaluate points lying on the efficient frontier. The result of this evaluation is usually a point (solution) on the efficient frontier, which pleases the DM most. The solution is called the DM's *Most Preferred Solution* (MPS). In Joro et al. (1998), we have shown that Multiple Objective Linear Programming models (MOLP-models) and DEA-models have a similar structure. Thus, theory and approaches developed in MCDM for evaluating solutions on the efficient frontier can also be applied in DEA. We can search for good solutions also on the efficient frontier in DEA.

The Most Preferred Solution plays a key role in the approach developed by Halme et al. (1999) to incorporate preference information into DEA. The approach is called *Value Efficiency Analysis* (VEA).

In the following, we review the main ideas of Value Efficiency Analysis. We also consider some extensions and further research topics.

14.3.1 Additional Details of Value Efficiency Analysis

The Value Efficiency Analysis consists of the following two phases:

1. Find the Most Preferred Solution (MPS) (= the solution which pleases you most) on the efficient frontier using a software developed for Multiple Objective Linear Programming
2. Find the value efficient coefficients for all units

For finding the MPS, you can use Pareto Race and its software VIG (Fig. 14.2), which makes it possible to freely search the efficient frontier.

To illustrate the Value Efficiency Analysis, we use our numerical data set in Table 14.2. First, we use Pareto Race to find the Most Preferred Solution. Because we have only two outputs, the search is quite easy, because it can be limited to a

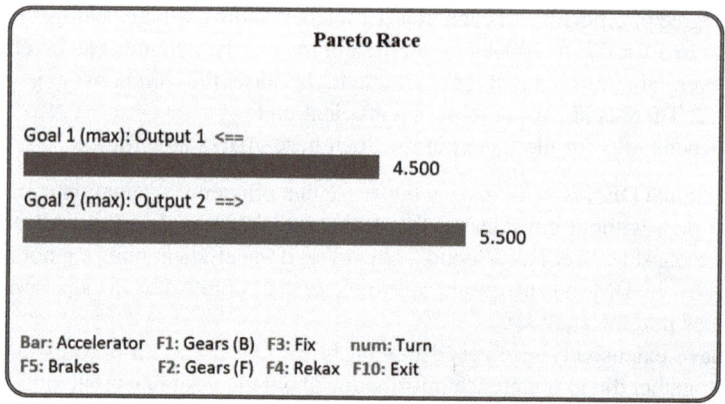

Fig. 14.2 Pareto race screen (most preferred solution)

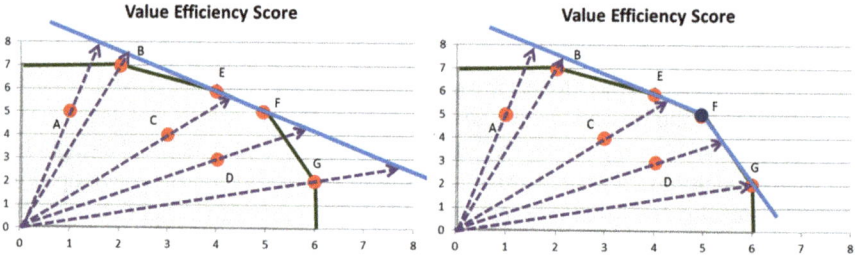

Fig. 14.3 Illustration of value efficiency analysis using data from Table 14.2

Table 14.4 Value efficiency scores and reference units, when MPS is on edge (EF)

Ref. units	A	B	C	D	E	F	G
B	0						
E	3.33	2.79	0.71	−0.71	1		−2.50
F	−2.33	−1.78	0.29	1.71		1	3.50
G							
ValEff. scores	0.600	0.900	0.700	0.700	1.000	1.000	0.800
Eff. scores	0.714	1.000	0.700	0.750	1.000	1.000	1.000

two-dimensional search from B to G.[8] Assume that the DM has identified as her Most Preferred Solution: Output 1 = 4.5 and Output 2 = 5.5, see the left-hand figure in Fig. 14.3 Based on the DM's MPS, the so-called value efficient frontier is computed. The value efficient frontier consists of all points, which could be at least as preferred as the MPS. Points which lie below the value efficient frontier are definitely less preferred than the MPS.

---

[8]The points left from B and down from G are weakly efficient.

Because the MPS lies on the edge (E to F), the value efficient frontier is the blue line, which goes through points E and F.

The computation of value efficiency scores is based on the radial projection of units onto the value efficient frontier. The closer a unit is to the value efficient frontier, the higher is its value efficiency score. The scores are given in Table 14.4. When we compare efficiency scores and value efficiency scores, we see that value efficiency scores are smaller than efficiency scores for A, B, D, and G. Unit B is technically efficient, but it is "too far" from the MPS (or more precisely from the value efficient frontier). The only value efficient units are E and F. We can also find reference units (benchmarks) for all other units.

Next, let us assume that the DM has specified that the MPS is unit F (the right figure in Fig. 14.3). Now the value efficient frontier is a cone. It is defined by vectors FG and FE. The edge from F to G belongs to the value efficient frontier. Unit G is value efficient and the value efficiency of D is the same as its technical efficiency. Unit B's value efficiency is the same for both Most Preferred Solutions.

Finally, consider the Value Efficiency Analysis of hypermarkets A, B, ..., D using the original data set in Table 14.1. Assume that the DM has named unit D as the Most Preferred Unit. Recall that unit B was the only not technically efficient unit. Its efficiency score was 0.932. When we carry out Value Efficiency Analysis for all units, B still remains the only unit which was not value efficient. Its value efficiency score is 0.927, which is a little bit worse than its above-mentioned technical efficiency score.

For readers who are mathematically inclined, and interested in learning more about Value Efficiency Analysis, we recommend the book by Joro and Korhonen (2015).

References

Charnes, A., Cooper, W. W., & Rhodes, E. (1978). Measuring efficiency of decision making units. *European Journal of Operational Research, 2*, 429–444.

Charnes, A., Cooper, W. W., & Rhodes, E. (1979). Short communication: measuring efficiency of decision making units. *European Journal of Operational Research, 3*, 339.

Cooper, W. W., Seiford, L. M., & Tone, K. (2007). *Data envelopment analysis: a comprehensive text with models. Applications, references and DEA-solver software* (2nd ed.). Boston: Kluwer Academic Publishers.

Emrouznejad, A., & Yang, G. (2018). A survey and analysis of the first 40 years of scholarly literature in DEA: 1978–2016. *Socio-Economic Planning Sciences, 61*(1), 4–8.

Halme, M., Joro, T., Korhonen, P., Salo, S., & Wallenius, J. (1999). A value efficiency approach to incorporating preference information in data envelopment analysis. *Management Science, 45*(1), 103–115.

Joro, T., & Korhonen, P. (2015). *Extension of data envelopment analysis with preference information: Value efficiency*. New York: Springer.

Joro, T., Korhonen, P., & Wallenius, J. (1998). Structural comparison of data envelopment analysis and multiple objective linear programming. *Management Science, 44*(7), 962–970.

Chapter 15
Real-World Problems

During our careers we have been involved as consultants in several real-world projects, sometimes together, sometimes separately, but often involving other people. Some of the problems have been corporate decision problems, some public sector decision problems.

One of our first consulting projects took place in mid-70's at S.A. Cockerill, a large Belgian steel company. Jyrki Wallenius and Stanley Zionts were involved in this study. Further details can be found in Wallenius and Zionts (1976). Our aim was to solve Cockerill's aggregate production planning problem. The problem had multiple objectives. We began with modeling their problem as a multiple objective Linear Programming problem, defining the feasible decision alternatives with the help of linear constraints (inequalities). Then we experimented with our brand-new interactive man-machine algorithm to solve the problem. Phases of computation would alternate with phases of decisions, during which the decision-maker guided the process by providing answers to yes-no tradeoff questions. The tradeoff questions were essentially directions, and the decision-maker was supposed to indicate whether he liked or did not like the direction of change. Our experiment did not lead to a large-scale real-world implementation, but we learned a lot from working with company people. The reader should realize that at that time there were no personal computers. Instead, Cockerill had a large mainframe computer. It was not trivial to interact with a mainframe computer!

Another early application took place at N.V. Philips Corporation, Eindhoven, The Netherlands, during late 1970's and early 1980's. Stanley Zionts and Jyrki Wallenius gave their interactive man-machine multi-objective algorithm for the company to use. Which they in fact did. They built a Linear Programming planning model (high-level) and over a period of seven years used our algorithm as part of the company's strategy planning process. When we wanted to learn about their experiences, they politely declined to talk to us.

In this chapter we will talk about a number of interesting both private and public sector applications, in which we have been involved.

15.1 Pricing Alcoholic Beverages

Korhonen and Soismaa (1988) discussed the problem of determining optimal price changes for alcoholic beverages in Finland. Finland has, in the style of Utah, a government sales monopoly for alcoholic beverages. The company in charge of selling alcoholic beverages is called Alko Ltd. The price decisions are among the most important alcohol policy measures, because with prices the government hopes to guide the consumers' purchasing decisions.

Alko Ltd. was somewhat in a schizophrenic situation, because at the same time they wanted to sell (to make money for the government) and not to sell (to minimize harmful effects on the population). Hence, the pricing problem was not only a profit maximization problem. Other relevant criteria (objectives) included the intention of reducing harmful effects due to alcohol consumption, and the minimization of the impact of price increases on the consumer price index. (Alcohol prices were part of the consumer price index.)

A multiple criteria model for finding the Most Preferred Solution for pricing alcoholic beverages in Finland was developed by Korhonen and Soismaa. The model included three criteria: profit (max), consumption of absolute alcohol (min), and impact of price changes on the consumer price index (min). The model included price elasticity data. The model could be solved by using any existing multiple criteria decision software. Korhonen and Soismaa used a visual interactive Goal Programming method developed by Korhonen and Laakso (1986), which is the continuous version of VIMDA described in a previous chapter. See also Korhonen and Wallenius Pareto Race (1988).

The Minister of Finance attended one of the demo sessions, implying The Finnish government's interest in the model and its implementation. On the basis of the prototype, Alko Ltd. did implement an extended version of the model. The model was solved by using our algorithm.

One of the conclusions was that Alko Ltd.'s situation was not quite as schizophrenic as it first appeared. The way to resolve the conflict between making money and reducing harmful effects of alcohol consumption was that the government should lower the prices of wines and increase the prices of heavy liquor. This started a trend, making Finnish people's drinking habits more in line with Continental Europe. At the time, Finns did not drink that much wine, but the working class had vodka drinking habits. However, the absolute alcohol consumption steadily increased in Finland until 2007. After that it has been decreasing.

15.2 Emergency Management

In collaboration with the National Board of Economic Defense, a government agency which has subsequently merged with another agency, we conducted a study about analyzing the consequences of various economic, natural, or political crises on the Finnish economy. Our collaborators were H. Wallenius and I. Kananen. Kananen worked in a leadership role at the agency and is the CEO of the new agency: National Emergency Supply Agency.

The structure of the Finnish economy was modelled with the help of a classic input-output model due to Leontief, a Nobel-laureate in economics. Input-output models describe the inter-industry relationships within an economy, thus allowing one to trace the dependencies of the different sectors in an economy (Input-Output models 1985).

We studied the quantitative effects of economic or political crises to the Finnish economy with the help of an input-output model pioneered by Osmo Forssell in Finland. Examples of such crises are many:

- nuclear power plant accidents
- energy crises
- trade embargoes
- crop failures, and
- various international conflicts.

We used an input-output model of the Finnish economy with 17 industries (sectors). We solved the model using our multi-objective technology, the Pareto Race. Our system was implemented on a microcomputer, and at the time it was being used and enhanced by the National Board of Economic Defense. Several different crisis scenarios were studied. Note that in our system, the decision-maker could influence the solution of the model, in other words how the consequences of a crisis are dealt with. Additional details about our study can be read from Kananen et al. (1990).

15.3 Cost Efficiency of Finnish Electricity Distributors

Pekka Korhonen conducted an interesting study, with his PhD student, Mikko Syrjänen, for the Ministry of Trade and Industry and the Energy Market Authority in Finland in early 2000 (Korhonen and Syrjänen 2003). Their study was about evaluating the cost-efficiency of Finnish electricity distribution companies for price regulation purposes. One of the tasks of the Authority is to define the cost level that a company can achieve if it operates efficiently. The "reasonable" price level can cover the "efficient cost" level and a reasonable return on investment.

In Finland, the Electricity Market Act freed the electricity markets in 1995. Under the new law, sales, production, transmission and distribution of electricity are separate functions. Transmission and distribution functions form natural monopolies. Accordingly, one distribution company is allowed to operate in each geographic region. According to the Electricity Market Act, the companies must provide electricity to all households in their region and do this for a reasonable price. Also, the companies must maintain and develop their network so that the needs of the customers are met. Moreover, the quality of the network must be adequate, measured via interruption time.

But what is a "reasonable" price and what is "adequate" quality? The Energy Market Authority, the customers, and the companies probably have a different view on this. The law obliges the Energy Market Authority to supervise the distribution business and the reasonableness of the pricing.

The efficiency evaluation was based on the use of Data Envelopment Analysis (DEA), which has been described in our book. The input variable was operational costs, and the output variables the amount of distributed energy and the quality of distribution (measured via interruption time). The numeric data for the input and output variables formed the basis for the efficiency analysis. By law, the companies were obliged to provide the authorities with this data.

We also wish to mention that Korhonen and Syrjänen went to considerable lengths to account for the fact that different companies operate in different environments (geographic locations). Otherwise the comparison would not be fair. In total, they studied the efficiency of 102 companies, 21 of which turned out to be efficient. The efficiency of the companies varied from 43% to 100%, averaging 77%.

The Energy Market Authority used for several years the model by Korhonen and Syrjänen in supervising the reasonableness of distribution pricing. Quite a few distribution companies also used a modified version of the model in evaluating their own efficiency.

15.4 Value Efficiency Analysis

In this subsection, we review several practical applications, in which Value Efficiency Analysis (VEA) was used.

15.4.1 Case 1: Hypermarkets

One of the first applications, in which we applied Value Efficiency Analysis was our hypermarket study. The aim was to help the management of Prisma chain (part of the S Group) evaluate and compare hypermarkets, which belonged to the same concern. Our colleague, Mr. Aapo Siljamäki, was involved in the study over several years during the 1990's.

The original application consisted of 25 hypermarkets. The number of outputs (Sales and Profits) and inputs (Man Hours and Floor Space) was two. Only four out of the 25 hypermarkets were technically efficient. The technically efficient markets remained Value Efficient. As we discussed before, the Value Efficiency score can never be better than the technical efficiency score. For instance, the technical efficiency of Market 11 was 92.0%, but its Value Efficiency score was 86.5% (unpublished consulting report by Siljamäki and Korhonen). Finland experienced a severe recession during the 90's. Interestingly, Prisma was the only supermarket chain that was profitable at the time. Siljamäki did extensive analysis work for the company. How they used the results of the analysis, we do not know.

15.4.2 Case 2: Academic Research

In the early 1990s the Ministry of Education in Finland signaled that government research funding would to a larger extent be allocated to universities demonstrating a good track record of high-quality research. This led the Research Development Group (TUTKE) at the Helsinki School of Economics (currently Aalto University, School of Business), chaired by the rector, to establish a two-person team[1] with the goal of developing an approach to evaluating research performance.

We viewed academic research as analogous to a production process in economics, having inputs and outputs. The analogy between research and production processes is not novel and some other authors—in the same spirit as we—have also proposed the use of DEA to evaluating research performance. Indeed, the presence of multiple outputs and their intangible nature makes this problem very well suited to DEA.

In total, 18 units were included in the study. Many of the units represented functional business school departments, such as Organization & Management, Accounting, Finance, Marketing, Logistics, etc.

The second step included the definition of criteria, which were to be used in measuring research performance of the units. After several discussion sessions, the Helsinki School of Economics ended up with the following final set of criteria (outputs):

- Quality of Research
- Research Activeness
- Impact of Research
- Activeness in Educating Young Scientists (especially doctoral students)

Moreover, for each criterion we introduced indicators, which were used to find numerical values for the criteria. Next, the indicators were aggregated using a weighted sums model. Our study included one input, namely the unit's budget.

Four out of the 18 units were technically efficient. We used Pareto Race to find the Most Preferred Solution (MPS) on the efficient frontier. The MPS reflected the preferences of the Vice Rector (for research). The units which defined the MPS were A and R, in which the weight for A was 0.748 and for R 0.252. Three out of four technically efficient units were also Value Efficient. The Value Efficiency of the (previously) technically efficient unit dropped from 1 to 0.45. The Rector of the Helsinki School of Economics used the model to allocate part of the school's funds

---

[1] We formed the two-person team.

to the departments. For additional details, see Korhonen, Tainio, and Wallenius (2001).

15.4.3 Case 3: Parishes

The Evangelical Lutheran Church is Finland's largest Church. By the end of 2018, 70% of Finns were members of the Church. The Helsinki area is divided into Finnish speaking religious parishes on a geographical basis. The parishes offer numerous services and organize various activities to their members. In early 2000, the number of Finnish speaking parishes in Helsinki was 24.

In the late 1990s and early 2000s, big changes took place in the financial administration of the parishes. An influential person (Vicar Siljamäki) within the Church contacted our colleague, Merja Halme, with the wish to introduce new financial thinking in the Church. Vicar Siljamäki had learned from his brother of Data Envelopment Analysis. He expressed an interest in co-operation with Merja Halme and Pekka Korhonen in order to apply the approach in the context of parishes. In our case study, he played the role of the DM. The actual analysis was carried out in 2002–2003.

Whereas the previous case dealing with academic research was a rather straightforward application of DEA, here the emphasis was not so much on efficiency scores, but in the reference set—benchmarks—that the analysis produced. The DM indicated that there was a great deal of heterogeneity among the parishes, and that it was crucial that the benchmarks of inefficient parishes share the same key environmental and demographic characteristics. It became obvious that the results from standard DEA were unsatisfactory from this point of view. We thought that Value Efficiency Analysis was a more appropriate approach to factor in heterogeneity. Our key idea was that by selecting for each unit a most preferred benchmark unit with similar key characteristics, the resulting reference set would yield more meaningful benchmark information.

As is probably the case in any major city, different areas seem to attract similar kinds of households. For instance, in areas where young families live, there is much demand for services for children and families, whereas different kinds of outputs are required in the areas inhabited mostly by middle-aged and retired people. Hence, it is not realistic to assume that all parishes are comparable without considering the heterogeneity of the environment.

We assumed that the DM was able to describe the heterogeneity of the units by nominating (efficient) example units (benchmarks). A benchmark unit may be any efficient existing (or virtual) unit. The benchmark units thus represent different facets/types of goodness of performance. These benchmarks are then used as Most Preferred Solutions in VEA.

As our approach considers the DM's preference information in the form of benchmarks, it does not require the quantification or even identification of the

15.4 Value Efficiency Analysis

sources of heterogeneity. If the DM is able to name example units (benchmarks) among the DMUs, they are interpreted as "best" in the set of certain types of units.

The basic idea of the analysis was as follows:

1. Name the benchmarks for certain types of units (three in total).
2. Assume that the benchmarks represent the Most Preferred Solutions for certain types of parishes.
3. Carry out Value Efficiency Analysis for each benchmark.

The following output variables were used in the analysis: number of people attending (1) (religious) services, (2) music and other events, (3) adults' and senior people's groups, (4) children's and young people's groups, as well as (5) number of contacts with social workers. As an input we used the available funds (€).

The DM used the results from the analysis in discussions within the Church. In the words of Vicar Siljamäki, "the numbers opened the eyes of many church stakeholders to see, among other things, that some of the parishes were getting more funds per output(s) than others". For additional details, please read Halme and Korhonen (2015).

15.4.4 Case 4: Bank Branch Efficiency

One of Pekka Korhonen's PhD students, Juha Eskelinen, wrote his dissertation about bank branch efficiency in a major Finnish bank (OP Pohjola Group). The study dealt with the turbulent years in the financial sector: 2007–2010. The study was conducted in collaboration with OP Pohjola group (Eskelinen 2014).

Traditional efficiency measurement schemes are value-free (such as original Data Envelopment Analysis). In contrast with that, the authors used Value Efficiency, a method developed by us together with colleagues, to measure bank branch efficiency (Halme et al. 1999). More specifically, Eskelinen asked the bank executives to identify their most preferred branch office and used that as the benchmark, against which efficiency was determined.

In total, 25 bank branches operating in the Helsinki metropolitan area were evaluated. The input measure was each unit's sales force and the output measures were the sales from financial services and from investment services. Financial services included housing loans and consumer loans. Investment services included advicing about savings plans, mutual funds, etc. Hence the efficiency of each branch was evaluated based on one input measure and two output measures. Basically, a unit is more efficient than another if it produces more outputs with the same inputs, or the same outputs with less inputs.

Such efficiency analyses are normally conducted for homogeneous (similar) units only. In the case of bank branch evaluation, the authors clustered the branches into 5 homogeneous groups and performed the analysis for each cluster separately. For example, the location greatly impacted the performance of a branch, and there is not much one can do about it, except close down branches in poor neighborhoods.

The study helped the bank further develop their network of branch offices. Smallest branch offices (5–7 people) tended to be outperformed by the mid-sized offices (8–10 people) in efficiency. The insight concerning the critical size led OP Pohjola Group to reorganize its existing branches. The study also led to increased collaboration between the branches. Moreover, the opening hours were revisited and extended.

References

Eskelinen, J. (2014). *Efficiency evaluation in a retail bank*. PhD Dissertation, Aalto University School of Business.

Halme, M., Joro, T., Korhonen, P., Salo, S., & Wallenius, J. (1999). A value efficiency approach to incorporating preference information in data envelopment analysis. *Management Science, 45*(1), 103–115.

Halme, M., & Korhonen, P. (2015). Using value efficiency analysis to benchmark non-homogeneous units. *International Journal of Information Technology and Decision Making, 14*(4), 727–745.

Input-output Models, Research Institute of the Finnish Economy (ETLA), Series B 46 (1985).

Kananen, I., Korhonen, P., Wallenius, H., & Wallenius, J. (1990). Multiple objective analysis of input-output models for emergency management. *Operations Research, 38*(2), 193–201.

Korhonen, P., & Laakso, J. (1986). A visual interactive method for solving the multiple criteria problem. *European Journal of Operational Research, 24*, 277–287.

Korhonen, P., & Soismaa, M. (1988). A multiple criteria model for pricing alcoholic beverages. *European Journal of Operational Research, 37*(2), 165–175.

Korhonen, P., & Syrjänen, M. (2003). Evaluation of cost efficiency in finnish electricity distribution. *Annals of Operations Research, 121*(1), 105–122.

Korhonen, P., Tainio, R., & Wallenius, J. (2001). Value efficiency analysis of academic research. *European Journal of Operational Research, 130*(1), 121–132.

Korhonen, P., & Wallenius, J. (1988). A Pareto Race. *Naval Research Logistics, 36*(6), 361–375.

Wallenius, J., & Zionts, S. (1976). Some tests of an interactive programming method for multicriterion optimization and an attempt at implementation. In G. Fandel & T. Gal (Eds.), *Multiple criteria decision making*. Heidelberg: Springer.

Chapter 16
Negotiating a Deal

Negotiation analysis is a field, which is closely related to Multiple Criteria Decision Making—the subject of our book. It is a fascinating field. Sometimes you just negotiate over price, but often there are multiple issues (criteria) involved. In a negotiation situation, the general feeling is that the negotiating parties will be better off by reaching (or trying to reach) a settlement (a joint agreement), rather than acting independently on their own. In the simplest case, there are only two parties. However, multi-party negotiations are not uncommon either.

In negotiating, we commonly talk either about win-lose or win-win situations. By win-lose negotiations we mean negotiations, which are literally about a fixed pie. What one party gains, the other loses. In win-win negotiations, there exist settlements or contracts which are better for everybody involved. It is always preferable to find win-win contracts, even though this may not be trivial. Sometimes there is a grey area. The negotiators treat the negotiations as win-lose, because they fail to perceive mutually beneficial contracts. We separate our discussion into win-lose and win-win negotiations.

Pon Staff writes in a Daily Blog on October 25th, 2016 in Harvard Law School Program on Negotiations: "It never hurts to learn from the past. Studying different negotiation examples can really help you figure out the methods that work for you." Then he presents 10 top negotiation examples, from which we all can learn. They are interesting and challenging negotiation examples, featuring many of the corporate leaders or world leaders.

There exist many excellent popular or practical negotiating texts, the purpose of which is to improve the reader's negotiating skills. One of the best-sellers is Fisher and Ury's *Getting to Yes* from 1981 (Fisher et al. 1991). Also see one of the author's Lecture Notes from a Negotiation Analysis Course (Wallenius 2019).

16.1 Win-Lose Negotiations

Win-lose negotiations are often about price, with everything else fixed. An example is a negotiation between a seller and a buyer. Think about wanting to buy a used car. Assume that we have visited several dealers representing the makes and models we are interested in. Let us further assume that we have a budget in mind (our reservation price), and that we have identified a car that we are interested in buying. However, the price is close to our reservation price, and we would like to see if the dealer can come with a better price (than shown on the car window).

Incidentally, it is a bad idea to reveal your reservation price to the dealer. One of the author's, when buying a year-old Jaguar X-type, made the mistake by letting the dealer know that he is not willing to pay more than 50,000 euros. He ended up paying 49,500! It is much better to let the dealer make the first serious offer, to which we react. The first offers (often called bids) are surprisingly important in win-lose negotiations. There is empirical evidence that quite frequently the price ends up being roughly half-way between the seller's and buyer's initial bids. During the process both parties must make concessions from their previous (or initial) positions. The process of making concessions is called a 'negotiation dance'.

Negotiations are hard work. You should spend time to learn to know the opposing negotiating party. What is their situation? Do they have good options, if our deal does not materialize? If we are the buyer, how badly does the seller want to sell (to us)? If she urgently needs the money, we should use this information as a bargaining chip. Even better (although this could be unrealistic), if we know the other party's reservation price.

Other useful practical negotiating advice follows.

- Give yourself enough room to make concessions
  If your initial bid is the same as your reservation price, there is no room for further concessions. The expectation in negotiations is that both parties make reasonable concessions.
- Try to get the other party to start revealing their needs and objectives first
  Even better, if you can find out about the other party's needs and objectives prior to the actual negotiations. If that is not possible, the first steps in negotiations may reveal valuable information about either party's needs and objectives. It makes sense to be rather passive and not too eager at first.
- Be the first to concede on a minor issue but not the first to concede on a major issue
  This strategy works if the negotiations involve more than one issue.
- Make unimportant concessions and portray them as more valuable than they are
  It is great if this strategy works. Sometimes, however, the other party might out-guess you.
- Make the other party work hard for every concession you make. Generally, concede slowly and do not give much with each concession.

Evidence shows that it is a good idea to alternate in concessions. Do not unilaterally make multiple concessions in a row, without requiring the other party to make any.

- Do not reveal your deadline to the other party
  This is a very important point. Generally, the party who is in a hurry to close a deal, looses.
- Occasionally "say no" to the other negotiator
  This shows that you are not a push-over.
- Keep a record of concessions made in the negotiation to try to identify a pattern
  This is a good idea, so that we do not forget the concessions each has made.

Use threats very selectively, in particular if there is an ongoing relationship between the parties. Most likely threats will backfire. In early January 2019 there was a US Government shutdown. President Trump threatened to keep the government shut as long as it takes, for months, or until the next elections, unless he gets the funding for the US Mexico border wall. The threat did not work very well.

To sum up, do not concede "too often, too soon, or too much". And do your due diligence (prior to the negotiations). Negotiations are hard work. Some are better at it than others. But we can all learn to be better negotiators.

16.2 Win-Win Negotiations

Particularly in negotiations, which involve multiple issues, one should always make a serious attempt to identify win-win settlements or contracts. It is not trivial, but we should try. Sometimes in politics a win-win settlement is created by an outside mediator. Raiffa describes the Egyptian-Israel peace negotiations in 1978, where US Secretary of State Cyrus Vance acted as the mediator on behalf of the US Government (Raiffa 2002, p. 321). To make a long story short, US exerted both pressure and offered financial aid to sweeten the deal. And the deal was struck.

The reason why we are able to identify win-win settlements in multi-issue negotiations is that the negotiating parties often value different issues differently. What is important to us, may be less important to the other side, and vice versa. For the win-win approach to work, we should one way or the other find out how the negotiating parties value the different issues.

Raiffa advocates the use of so-called templates. A template lists the issues and their (resolution) levels. We illustrate with a labor-management negotiation. Assume that the City Police is negotiating with the City about increases in monthly salaries for police officers (issue 1), possible increases in vacation days per year (issue 2), and whether officers have the right to bear arms when patrolling night-time (issue 3). The resolution levels of the issues are described in Table 16.1.

Raiffa next suggests that both parties give importance scores to each issue, including the different (resolution) levels. The scores for a party should add up to 100.

Table 16.1 Template

Issue	Resolution
Salary increase	0
	200
	400
Extra vacation days	0 days
	2 days
	4 days
Right to bear arms	No
	Yes

Let us assume that the police officers (who feel that they are relatively well paid) provide the following scores for salary increases: 0 (increase 0), 10 (increase 200), 20 (increase 400); for vacation days: 0 (0 days), 20 (2 days), 30 (4 days); and the right to bear arms: 0 (no), 20 (yes). The City's budget is tight; hence they prefer no salary increases: 40 points for 0 salary increase; 10 points for 200 salary increase; and 0 points for 400 salary increase. The City's value scores for additional vacation days are 0 (0), 20 (2), and 20 (4); and 0 for no rights to bear arms, 10 for rights to bear arms.

The police officers highly value extra vacation days, and in fact both parties are in favor of the officers having the right to bear arms at night. The situation is such that win-win possibilities arise. We will show how to find them.

There are 18 possible contracts, because issue 1 has 3 levels, issue 2 has 3 levels, and issue 3 has 2 levels. The product of 3 times 3 times 2 is 18. However, notice that 9 of the contracts are uninteresting, that is where issue 3 is at level 'no' (both parties value the 'yes' option higher). The joint values of the 9 interesting contracts are depicted in Fig. 16.1. The scores of the police officers are on the x-axis and the scores of the City on the y-axis.

Contracts (50,70), (60,40), and (70,30) are so called efficient contracts, which can be found in the north-east corner. It does not make sense to settle on any of the other contracts, because both parties can do better. Which of the three efficient contracts is the fairest? The answer depends on our definition of fairness. The theorists favor two definitions. Either the maximum of the product of the scores, which suggests the first contract among the three efficient ones (the product of the scores is maximum 3500). Or the maximum of the minimum scores, which again points to the first contract. In our case, both fairness criteria suggest the same contract. This contract may or may not be chosen, depending on the negotiating power of the parties, and how truthful (and able) they have been when expressing the scores.

16.3 Pre-Negotiations Are Useful

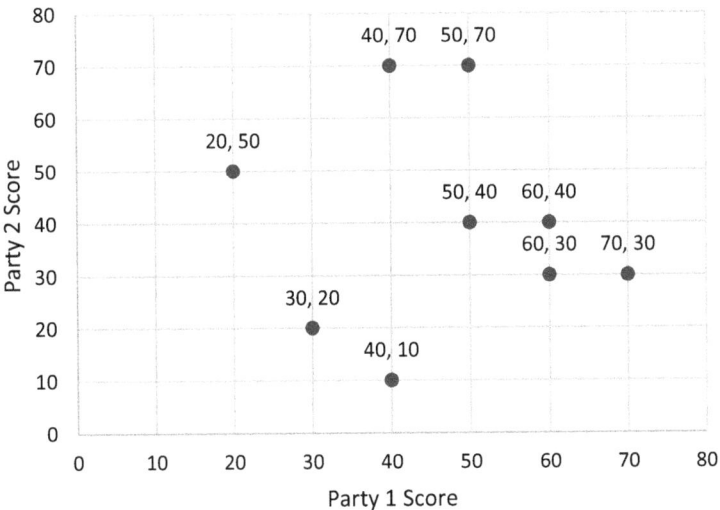

Fig. 16.1 Joint Values of 9 Contracts

16.3 Pre-Negotiations Are Useful

Two former PhD students of ours from the Helsinki School of Economics, Johanna Bragge (nee Pajunen) and Raimo Voutilainen, conducted as part of their PhD dissertations a real-world pre-negotiation analysis. Raiffa calls such negotiations with surrogate negotiators pseudo-mock negotiations. They are often extremely helpful to learn of each other's interests and setting the stage for the actual negotiations, or just improving our understanding of the conflict.

Bragge's study dealt with the energy taxation dispute in Finland in 1990's. For her surrogate negotiators she used representatives of the Confederation of Finnish Industries and well-known environmentalists, among others, from the Green Party. Voutilainen's dissertation was about trying to find the best alliance structure between banks and insurance companies, a topic that has gained world-wide interest during last decade. His surrogate negotiators in one study were leaders of major Finnish banks and insurance companies, and in a sequel study, regulators.

A useful concept not only in pre-negotiations, but also in actual negotiations is the Best Alternative To a Negotiated Agreement, for short BATNA. BATNA tells us the best alternative for each party, in case the negotiations fail. It is highly useful, although not necessarily easy, to know one's BATNA, let alone the other party's BATNA. In negotiations, you should never settle below your BATNA. Why would you?

Bragge, following Raiffa, provides advice on the steps that one should follow to conduct a useful pre-negotiation analysis.

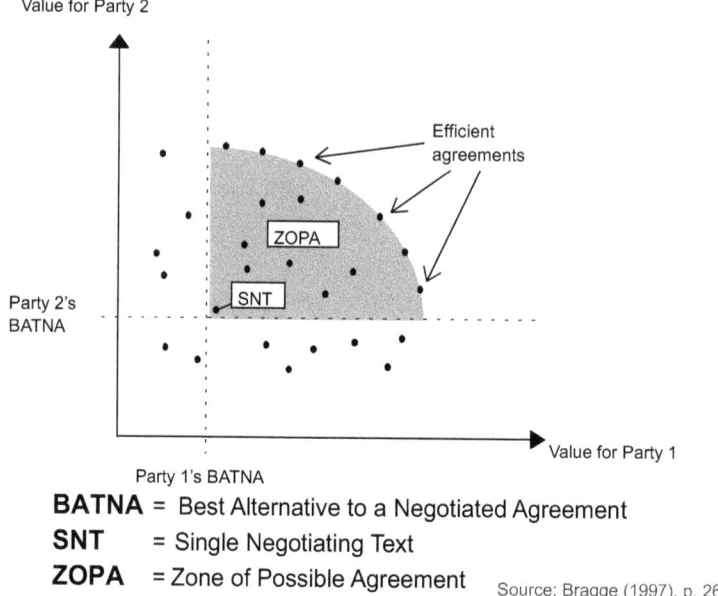

Fig. 16.2 BATNA, SNT, ZOPA

1. Document (neutrally) the history of the dispute.
2. Analyze the interests of the disputing parties, and provide a quantitative analysis of their preferences.
3. Identify efficient agreements.
4. Identify the no-agreement zone (including Best Alternative to Negotiated Agreement (BATNA), and Zone of Possible Agreement (ZOPA), which by definition exceeds the parties' BATNAs.
5. Suggest a starting point for the negotiations (Single Negotiating Text (SNT)), which hopefully will be improved during the negotiations (see Fig. 16.2 BATNA, SNT, ZOPA).

16.4 Real-World Examples

We provide some additional details of the Bragge and Voutilainen studies below.

The Bragge study had a direct impact on the government energy policy for year 1997. It also helped pave the way for future energy taxes and increased both side's understanding of each other's goals. The compromise deal reached implied a FIM 1,1 billion raise in energy taxes and equivalent income tax cuts for 1997.

The Voutilainen study enhanced our understanding of different bank-insurance company alliances, and it helped bank and insurance bosses more clearly see the pros

16.4.1 To What Extent Should Energy Be Taxed?

Taxation of energy has been a hot topic in many Western countries for over two decades. The aim of environment-related energy taxes (applied to fuels and electricity) is to encourage energy savings and provide incentives for the production and use of cleaner energy sources. Of particular concern are the CO_2 emissions.

The arguments of the environmentalists include promoting sustainable growth, simply saving the planet for future generations. The main arguments of the industrialists state that energy taxes hamper competitiveness of the industry, and competitiveness of the country. In Finland, at the time, 75% of exports were for energy-intensive products. Moreover, the industry's energy tax burden was triple from EU average at the time. To make matters worse, 8 firms paid over 75% of such taxes.

Bragge applied the so-called Single Negotiating Text (SNT) approach to negotiations (Bragge 1997, 2019, also see Raiffa 1985). The idea is to start from a not so good solution for everybody (SNT in Fig. 16.2), and then systematically, stepwise improve upon the initial SNT. In her study, she led her surrogates (two industrialists and two environmentalists) to work out the objectives for each party. Then, the negotiating parties developed a template for the problem, that is listed all the issues important to them, including different resolution levels. In total, six issues were identified. They all possessed a couple of resolution levels. The issues were.

1. What tax-model is used (75/25 model of year 1995, implying that 75% of energy taxes are based on CO_2 emissions and 25% on energy content, or a variation of it; or the 50/50 model applied in EU at the time)?
2. Estimated (energy) tax yield in 2000
3. To what extent are labor taxes lowered?
4. How is industry's competitiveness assured (with the possibility to (partially) compensate the industry)?
5. Are further incentives provided?
6. How are other income effects alleviated?

The problem was complex, including in total 648 energy taxation alternatives. Next, Bragge elicited the parties' preference tradeoffs, and their BATNAs. This allowed her to identify efficient contracts for the negotiations. Out of the 648 alternative contracts, roughly 20 were efficient. Note, however, that efficient is not the same as fair.

During the pre-stage negotiations, the surrogate negotiators were kept separate from each other.

After the pre-stage, Bragge acted as a neutral, but active mediator in actual surrogate negotiations between the parties. She constructed a starting SNT, which was improved upon 4 times. An agreement was finally reached among the surrogate negotiators. In a nutshell, it included keeping the basic 75/25 model as is, but amending it so that electricity's CO_2 tax is halved and a consumption tax is put into use for energy. Further, energy-intensive industry which is in open competition, will be given refunds from the energy taxes.

However, that was not the end of the story. Bragge published (with consent of the parties) the results of her study, which in fact affected the Finnish Government's budget for 1997. The case was a beautiful example of the power of pre-negotiations, in particular for situations where the parties have never before attempted to systematically understand each other's positions.

16.4.2 Should Banks and Insurance Companies Merge?

Voutilainen's dissertation dealt with different forms of collaboration between banks and insurance companies, in particular different kinds of alliances (Voutilainen 2006; Korhonen and Voutilainen 2006). It is natural that in the past there has been both competition and collaboration between banks and insurance companies. A recent phenomenon has been blurring of the old boundaries between banks and insurance companies.

Voutilainen classifies different alliance structures into three groups:

1. Cross-selling agreements, either with or without overlapping service channels. Cross-selling means that the parties agree to sell each other's products to their own customers. Most often a bank sells insurance products to their own customers.
2. Alliance of independent partners, either with or without overlapping service channels. In this case the alliance is strengthened by cross or joint ownership, implying a minority stake in the other company.
3. Control by ownership, either a bank owning an insurance company or vice versa; or a holding company owning banks and insurance companies.

Moreover, together with bank and insurance bosses, he came up with nine criteria to compare different alliance (or collaboration) structures. We briefly list them:

1. Maximize the efficiency of new product development.
2. Implement the one service-point (or one-stop) principle as effectively as possible.
3. Find good compromises between conflicting earnings logics.
4. Maximize the efficiency of Customer Relationship Management
5. Optimize synergies from alliances (cost and revenue).
6. Minimize channel conflicts.
7. Secure sufficient solvency.
8. Maximize power from alliance as investor.
9. Maximize the efficiency of sales management.

Using pairwise comparisons, Voutilainen used the Analytic Hierarchy Process to find out the relative importance weights for the different criteria. In one of the negotiations, bank and insurance bosses jointly answered the pairwise comparisons. In other words, if they originally had a different idea about the relative importance of a criterion, they discussed the situation until they found a compromise. The compromise value was used as the input to the Analytic Hierarchy Process.

Next, the participants jointly compared the various alliance models on each criterion (separately). The synthesis generated scores for the different alliance structures, representing joint preferences of both sides. The most preferred alliance structure was number 3 above (holding company) and the second most preferred structure was also number 3 (bank owning an insurance company or vice versa).

In a follow-up meeting, some of the less important criteria were deleted, and some new criteria were added. The new criteria reflected economies of scale and scope. The initial sessions had failed to address risk; however, discussion of the riskiness of different options was subsequently considered important. Interestingly, as a result, the rank order of the best alliance structures did not change.

References

Bragge, J. (1997). *Premediation analysis of the energy taxation dispute in Finland.* PhD Dissertation, Helsinki School of Economics.

Bragge, J. (2019). *Lecture notes in negotiation analysis course (guest lecture).* Aalto University School of Business.

Fisher, R., Ury, W., & Patton, B. (1991). *Getting to yes: Negotiating agreement without giving in* (2nd ed.). New York: Penguin.

Korhonen, P., & Voutilainen, R. (2006). Finding the most preferred alliance structure between banks and insurance companies. *European Journal of Operational Research, 175*(2), 1285–1299.

Raiffa, H. (1985). Mock pseudo-negotiations with surrogate disputants. *Negotiation Journal, 1*(2), 111–115.

Raiffa, H., & (with J. Richardson and D. Metcalfe). (2002). *Negotiation analysis.* Boston, MA: Harvard University Press.

Voutilainen, R. (2006). In search for the best alliance structure between banks and insurance companies. PhD Dissertation, Helsinki School of Economics.

Wallenius, J. (2019). *Lecture notes in negotiation analysis course.* Aalto University School of Business.

Chapter 17
In Conclusion

This book is about decision-making. More specifically, this book is about how to make better decisions. We conclude our book by summarizing our advice, how you can improve your decision-making. Our advice is equally valid for corporate contexts and personal decisions.

17.1 Realize That Intuition May Fail You

In 2019 we did not experience a white Christmas in Helsinki. A common reaction of people was that this was due to the climate change and global warming. According to the climate scientists, it is highly likely that the climate change is human-induced. However, in this case people were barking at the wrong tree. They were using the wrong (intuitive) argument to further a good cause. Statistically, in Helsinki one-third of the Christmases are 'black'. Hence, 'black' Christmases are not rare. Another thing is that in the long run, we may experience more 'black' Christmases in the future as a result of global warming.

17.2 If Possible, Complement Your Intuition with Some Analysis

Sometimes the required analysis is simple, sometimes more complicated. Note, however, that more analysis is not necessarily always better. When thinking about how much decision support is desirable for you, think in terms of a cost-benefit analysis. What are the benefits from further analysis, and what are its (monetary and other) costs? Think whether the Benjamin Franklin type of decision approach is sufficient for you, or whether you need something more elaborate.

17.3 Be Aware of Common Decision Traps

Be aware of decision traps and biases, such as the confirming evidence bias, the anchoring bias, the status-quo bias, or the framing bias. Use a devil's advocate to test the soundness of your ideas. Listen to advice which challenges your original vision. Do not anchor your advisers! Bridges undergo feasibility tests. Then why not important corporate or personal decisions? Forewarned is forearmed!

17.4 Humans Focus on Differences

Tversky and Kahneman have established that humans focus on differences (from a reference alternative), less to absolute quantities. Loss aversion, that is the phenomenon that humans react more strongly to negative than to positive stimuli of the same magnitude, is an equally established fact. Be aware of the role of the reference point in decision-making.

17.5 Think Hard About All Possible Decision Alternatives

Be creative! Ask yourself, whether you have identified all viable decision alternatives, and given them due consideration. This is highly important, in particular if you have not identified truly excellent alternatives to choose from. In recruiting situations, the recruiting officer must constantly think, whether to settle for the so far best applicant, or whether to sample some more. Note that if you extend your sample, it will delay the decision process, and you may lose some of the original candidates.

17.6 Think Whether You Are 'Optimizer' or 'Satisficer'

How high is the cost for you of continuing the search (for better alternatives)?

17.7 Be Transparent About the Criteria

Have you listed all decision-relevant criteria or are there hidden criteria? Sometimes decision-makers on purpose hide some of the criteria. Moreover, do not ignore qualitative criteria, just because they are harder to measure than quantitative criteria. The criteria do matter, and so does the scale in which they are measured.

Note that not all criteria are in conflict, unless we are comparing alternatives at the nondominated frontier. Examples are maximizing sales or profits and minimizing costs. One of our guidelines is that, try to figure out whether you have reached the nondominated frontier or not.

17.8 Identify Dominated Decision Alternatives and Eliminate Them

It is not wise to choose a dominated alternative, because you can do better. For the concept of dominance to be meaningful, all criteria must be explicitly stated and measured on at least an ordinal scale. According to our experience, managers need help in identifying dominated alternatives. We think this is true in particular for so-called design problems, where the feasible alternatives have been defined via mathematical constraints, but to a lesser extent also for other (simpler) problems.

17.9 Think How You Want to Express Your Preferences

Be suspicious of 'importance' weights. Realize that a bigger weight does not necessarily imply bigger importance. Note that weights and scales, in which the criteria are measured, go hand in hand. We like pairwise comparisons! Use pairwise comparisons to estimate weights.

17.10 Think About Ways to Visualize Decision Alternatives

Think whether visualization brings added value. Be aware of, how people lie with statistics and support their views by 'appropriate' visual graphs. If your y-axis does not start at 0, it is easy to exaggerate the recent developments say in unemployment in either direction. This may be in your interest or not.

17.11 Improving Efficiency of Operations

There are excellent tools to help managers evaluate the efficiency of sub-units of their company. If technical efficiency is not enough, there are options, which incorporate the decision-maker's preferences into efficiency measurement.

17.12 Use Scenarios When Facing Uncertainty

Use scenarios to present several alternative future developments. Realize that if you are not comfortable assessing (subjective) probabilities, Scenario Analysis can be used without probabilities.

17.13 Figure Out What You Want and What the Other Party Wants

Identify and improve your Best Alternative To Negotiated Agreement (BATNA). In addition, try to estimate the other party's BATNA. Even better, if you can influence it. Identify win-win opportunities!

In order to do that, you must understand what you want and what the other party wants. You can do this informally by telling the other party what you want to achieve. Or you can do this formally by assigning scores to different resolution levels of issues. A general advice is to read one of the popular negotiation texts to improve your negotiation skills. Such books are usually good, in particular if written by academics.

Author Index

A
Alpert, M., 39
Andrews, D., 63, 67, 68, 72, 73, 111
Arbel, A., 16
Assad, A., 94, 101

B
Balakrishnan, N., 59
Belton, V., 115
Bowerman, B.L., 66
Bradfield, R., 122
Bragge, J., 118, 153–156

C
Camerer, C., 27
Charnes, A., 12, 94, 132
Chernoff, H., 63, 67, 68, 71–73, 111
Cooper, W.W., 12, 94, 132, 136

D
Dershowitz, A.M., 42
Devlin, K., 121

E
Edwards, E., 12
Emrouznejad, A., 136
Eskelinen, J., 147

F
Ferguson, R., 94
Fisher, R., 57, 149
Fisher, R.A., 67
Forssell, O., 143
Franklin, B., 75

G
Gass, S., 94, 101
Gigerenzer, G., 5
Good, I.J., 42

H
Halme, M., 137, 147
Hammond, J., 31, 35, 36, 39, 76
Hogarth, R., 121
Huff, D., 69

I
Ignizio, J.P., 94
Isaacson, W., 76

J
Joro, T., 137, 139

K
Kahneman, D., 5, 13, 25, 31, 36, 39
Kananen, I., 143

Kasanen, E., 3
Keen, P., 12
Keeney, R., 31, 35, 36, 39, 48
Köksalan, M., 115
Kontula, J., 112
Korhonen, P., 12, 25, 29, 66, 105, 111, 112, 114, 139, 142, 143, 146, 147

L
Laakso, J., 105, 114
Lee, S.M., 94
Levine, D.M., 64
Lotfi, V., 115

M
March, J., 4
Markowitz, 126
Maslow, A., 12
Miller, G., 52
Montibeller, G., 33
Moore, J.H., 59
Moskowitz, H., 25, 29, 54

N
Newton, I., 5

P
Peiponen, P., 112

R
Raiffa, H., 1, 31, 35, 36, 39, 46, 48, 57, 151
Rhodes, E., 132
Rosenhead, J., 33
Ruutu, J., 87

S
Saaty, T.L., 50, 75, 84, 101

Santalainen, T., 66
Scott-Morton, M., 12
Simon, H., 12, 21
Smith, L.I., 66
Soismaa, M., 142
Somervuori, O., 27
Steuer, R., 97, 115
Stewart, T.J., 115
Syrjänen, M., 143

T
Tainio, R., 66, 146
Tone, K., 136
Tversky, A., 12, 24, 25, 31, 36, 39

U
Ury, W., 149
Vilkkumaa, E., 122

V
Von Winterfeldt, D., 33
Voutilainen, R., 153, 154, 156

W
Wallenius, H., 3, 143
Wallenius, J., 3, 12, 25, 29, 33, 102–104, 114, 137, 141, 142, 146
Weatherford, L.R., 59
Wierzbicki, A., 104
Wright, G., 54

Y
Yang, G., 136

Z
Zeleny, M., 83
Zionts, S., 3, 12, 102–104, 141

Subject Index

A
Alternatives, 15
Analytic approach, 13
Analytic Hierarchy Process (AHP), 51, 84
Anchoring, 35
Andrews curves, 63
Artificial intelligence (AI), 6
Aspiration level, 22
Attributes, 50

B
Background context, 33
Bar charts, 63
BATNA, 153
Behavioral decision theory, 12
Benchmarks, 135
Benjamin Franklin's approach, 76
Biases, 12
Bi-criteria, 14
Bi-objective, 94
Bounded rationality, 12, 21
Boxplots, 66

C
Certainty, 53–55
Chernoff faces, 63
Choice-based paradigm, 1
Compensatory models, 21, 23
Comprehensive Capital and Analysis Review (CCAR), 124
Computer graphics, 63
Concave, 28

Conditional probabilities, 9
Confirming evidence trap, 31
Consequences table, 78
Convex, 28
Criteria, 15, 49
Criterion space, 97
Cycles, 29

D
Data Envelopment Analysis (DEA), 132
Decision, 16
Decision alternatives, 45
Decision-maker (DM), 1, 15, 16
Decision Making Unit (DMU), 133
Decision problem, 11
Decision Support Systems, 12
Decision variables, 45–46
Decision variable space, 97
Decoy, 34
Dependence, 51
Descriptive statistics, 63
Design, 91
Design problems, 57, 101–110
Devil's advocate, 2
Dodd-Frank Act stress tests (DFAST), 124
Dominance, 55–56
Dominated, 13, 18

E
Ebbinghaus illusion, 9
Elimination by aspects, 21, 24
Emergency Management, 142–143

Energy Market Authority, 143
Evaluation problem, 57
Even swaps, 76
Excel solver, 59
Expected state of affairs, 26
Expected utility, 1
Expected value (EV), 54
Expert systems, 4

F
Feasibility test, 2
Feasible set, 15
Final choice, 16
Framing, 36

G
Goal programming, 94
Goals, 49
Group decision-making, 57

H
Harmonious houses, 111–112
Heuristics, 12
Hidden criterion, 19
Hubris, 37

I
Importance scores, 151
Importance weights, 79
Indicators, 50
Input-output model, 143
Interactive, 12
Intuition, 5
Investment problem, 126

L
Lexicographic model, 21, 22
Linear programming, 12
Line graphs, 63
Local context, 33
Loss aversion, 26

M
Mathematical programming, 101
Most Preferred Solution (MPS), 16

Multidimensional scaling (MDS), 66
Multiple Criteria Decision Making (MCDM), 1, 13
Multiple Criteria Design, 15
Multiple criteria evaluation problem, 15
Multiple issues, 151
Multiple Objective Linear Programming (MOLP), 93, 117
Myopic problem representation, 32

N
National Board of Economic Defense, 142
Negotiation analysis, 149
Nondominated, 18, 34

O
Objective probabilities, 121
Objectives, 49
Operations research, 12
Optical illusion, 8
Optimal stopping rule, 46
Over-confidence, 37

P
Pairwise comparisons, 84
Pareto Race, 107
Path dependence, 29
Pie charts, 63
Preference, 12
Premature stopping, 29
Pricing, 142
Principal component analysis (PCA), 66
Production planning, 58, 115
Productivity, 131
Prospect theory, 12, 25
Prospect theory value function, 28
Prudence trap, 38
Pseudo-mock negotiations, 153
Psychology of decision making, 12

R
Radial, 136
Rational, 13
Rational man, 12
Recallability trap, 40
Reference direction, 87
Reference Direction Approach, 106

Subject Index

Reference point, 25
Reference Point Method, 104
Reference units, 135
Reflection effect, 26
Relative importance scale, 84
Risk averse, 26
Riskless choice, 1
Risk prone, 26
Rule-based decision-making, 3

S
Scatter plots, 64
Scenario, 13
Scenario analysis, 122
Secretary problem, 47
Settlement, 149
Single Negotiating Text (SNT), 154
Single-objective, 12
Status-quo, 26, 35
Subjective probabilities, 121
Sunk cost syndrome, 36
System 1, 6, 13
System 2, 13

T
Tradeoff, 16
Tradeoff aversion, 16
Transitivity, 118

U
Uncertainty, 53–55
Utility, 56

V
Value, 56
Value Efficiency Analysis (VEA), 137
Value function, 28
VICO, 112
Virtual inputs, 131
Virtual outputs, 131
Vision-based decision-making, 2–3
Visual interactive goal (VIG), 114
Visual Interactive Method for Discrete
    Alternatives (VIMDA), 87, 112
Visualization, 63

W
Weighted sums, 101–103
Weighting model, 23
Win-lose, 149
Win-win, 149
Wise decision, 16

Z
Zionts and Wallenius Algorithm, 102
Zone of Possible Agreement (ZOPA), 154

GPSR Compliance

The European Union's (EU) General Product Safety Regulation (GPSR) is a set of rules that requires consumer products to be safe and our obligations to ensure this.

If you have any concerns about our products, you can contact us on

ProductSafety@springernature.com

In case Publisher is established outside the EU, the EU authorized representative is:

Springer Nature Customer Service Center GmbH
Europaplatz 3
69115 Heidelberg, Germany

www.ingramcontent.com/pod-product-compliance
Lightning Source LLC
LaVergne TN
LVHW050013270326
834688LV00068B/36